Other Gateway Books by John Howells

Choose Costa Rica, 2nd ed. (1994)

Choose Mexico, 4th ed. (1994), with Don Merwin

Choose Spain (1990)

RV Travel in Mexico (1989)

Where to Retire (1995)

Coming in Spring 1996: *Choose the Southwest*

RETIREMENT ON A SHOESTRING

JOHN HOWELLS

Printed in the United States of America

Gateway Books

Distributed by Publishers Group West

10 9 8 7 6 5 4 3 2 1

Contents

Chapter One

Golden Retirement Years

When people speak of retirement, the phrase "golden years" commonly comes to mind. Golden, because these years are considered to be a reward—a substantial reward for a lifetime of productive work and loyalty to the company. Most workers eagerly look forward to these happy years as the time when they can enjoy the fruits of their labor and bask in the sunshine of leisure. A company pension, stock dividends, annuities, interest on savings, plus Social Security, provide the income to enjoy this new, carefree career as a retiree.

Unfortunately, not everyone has a company pension to cushion their golden years. Not everyone has had the good fortune to build up an investment portfolio that pays lavish dividends. For all too many, the main source of retirement dollars will be Social Security benefits. When Social Security checks do arrive, they're often dismally inadequate. To be fair, we must recognize that Social Security was never designed as a retirement fund, but rather as a supplement to retirement. But in real life, many retirees depend upon Social Security as their main source of income.

The worst-case scenarios are those folks who thought they were adequately covered for retirement only to discover that their retirement plans went south when their employers went bankrupt. Others, who invested heavily in savings and loan retirement bonds, find they are holding worthless paper for all their years of thrift. A friend of ours—a minister in a small-town church—invested his savings and much of his meager income into an insurance annuity. Then, just before his planned retirement, the promised $20,000-a-year annuity disappeared into the insurance company's bankruptcy proceedings. The company had traded his retirement money for junk bonds. In the closing years of the 20th century, pension plan failures and insurance annuity bankruptcies could surpass the 1980s savings and loan scandals.

Many retirees depend upon investments, interest on bank certificates of deposit and stock dividends to add to retirement income. But interest rates fluctuate, and utility dividends have slumped for the first time in decades. Even in a booming economy, income tends to decline as people age. And although the economy seems to be recovering from a long recession, it isn't exactly booming.

It isn't just those on Social Security who need to plan on getting by on a shoestring. Workers forced into early retirement because of corporate mergers or industrial doldrums won't qualify for Social Security until they reach retirement age. Other workers, whose skills or crafts have been eliminated by modern technology, often have no hope of finding new jobs. All of the above are forced to live on savings and income from part-time jobs. Therefore, this book tries to present strategies for maximizing the use of scarce retirement dollars for everybody, no matter what their level of income or how high their current net worth.

Retirement on a Shoestring

While my wife and I do our research to update and write new retirement books, we drive coast to coast, zig-zagging back and forth in search of desirable places to retire. We travel many thousands of miles by car, motorhome, fifth-wheel travel trailer and airline. As we visit cities, towns and hamlets, we try to imagine ourselves actually living in each place. Routinely, we look at rentals and property for sale and check prices in stores and restaurants. We examine newspaper classified sections for prevailing wages and mobile homes for sale. In each location, we estimate how much income the average retired couple would need to live there. Early on, we discovered that the cost of living varies markedly from region to region.

One day, as we were having lunch in a small city on Washington's coast, we began wondering what we could do on a minimum budget. After all, millions of U.S. retirees do live below the poverty level. What if our worst fears were realized, our only income a Social Security check? (If you're retiring in 1995 at age 65, with present annual earnings of $20,000, you'll probably receive $748 per month. If you are married, and your spouse is also 65, the check will be about $1,123.) Although an income of this magnitude would barely cover rent in many towns we've researched, we began to wonder: suppose we were to choose to retire here, in this little coastal community, could we survive? And at what standard of living?

We checked a real estate office for their cheapest listings and found an older, two-bedroom frame house in town selling for $20,000 and another outside of town, an older ranchhouse style home, for $32,000. Don't misunderstand: we're not suggesting that you can go just anywhere and pick up a house for $20,000! These houses were priced exceptionally low because the town's two major industries had closed, jobs had disappeared, and small businesses were struggling to survive. Houses were difficult to peddle because everyone wanted to sell and nobody wanted to buy. Empty houses weren't renting because tenants were moving away to seek work elsewhere. For retirees, however, employment opportunities don't matter nearly as much as affordable housing costs.

We located the first house—a slightly run-down place, not too far from a supermarket. As you can imagine, it needed paint, cleaning and undetermined repairs. Yet the house still looked like a bargain at $20,000. Yes, we could easily imagine ourselves living here, and the price was affordable, even considering the needed repairs. But suppose we couldn't afford to buy a house and needed to rent? The local newspaper listed several rentals for as little as $175 a month, some furnished.

We figured out a tentative "bare bones" budget for living modestly but comfortably in this town and came up with a figure of $830. The table below shows how we arrived at this figure. Automobile expenses accounted for $110. While car expenses might seem like a big chunk out of the budget, living here without a car would be difficult. (This is true of most small towns without local or intercity bus service.) Of course, this budget doesn't allow for items like automobile depreciation, life insurance premiums, club dues or loan payments or other expenses that vary with individual circumstances. Also, because the town's ocean-tempered climate is cool year-round, there's no need for air conditioning, and heating demands are minimal. Assuming that we could qualify for Medicare, and given the fact that our car is paid for and that we've already cashed in our life insurance, we added $60 for supplementary medical insurance. Yes, we could make all of our basic expenses on Social Security! That amount wouldn't begin to cover even rent and utilities in many other towns we've visited!

Rent, small 2-bdr	$175
Food	$225
Utilities	$60
Cable TV	$20
Automobile gas & maint.	$55
Automobile insurance	$55
Clothing, laundry, grooming	$70
Medicare supplement	$60
Miscellaneous	$110
Total	**$830**

Please note that throughout this book the cost of living refers only to basic expenses, those items most people say they cannot avoid. Obviously, individual circumstances differ. To our sample budgets you'll need to add your own extras. When you retire, if you still have car payments, mortgage payments, medical insurance, back taxes, alimony, gambling debts and serious bar tabs, you don't need a book on how to retire on a minimum income. You need a book on how to win the lottery. For those of you without medical coverage, you don't need someone telling you that you are in trouble. Until Congress, insurance companies and the medical establishment stop scratching each others' backs and permit our system to catch up with the rest of the world in assuring medical care for its citizens, millions of Americans will be without protection. Hopefully, you're one of those lucky enough to afford the care you need. If not, what can I say? You have plenty of company.

Home Base

At first glance, a small coastal town such as the one we were researching would appear to be a great place to retire. With wooded hills, a lazy river and lovely seascapes, summers here are delightful. Temperatures rarely rise above 75 degrees, and sunny days invite residents outside to enjoy the season. However, even though winters rarely bring even a hint of snow, residents complain about long, damp and overcast days with shortened daylight hours. Some might like this, but our personal tastes lean toward sunny winters where we can wear bathing suits instead of rain-coats. Another problem is the lack of community services for senior citizens. Towns where population and taxpayers are dwindling sometimes have few funds left over for retirement centers. This is an all-important consideration, as we shall see later on in this book.

Even though we recognized that this town was not the perfect retirement setting for us, we became interested in the possibility of using it as a "home base." The home's wide lot would make a great place to store our small motorhome while we enjoyed an inexpensive summer and fall, living in a peaceful, ocean setting. When winter rain and gloom threatened, we could store our things, winter-proof the house and drive our motorhome to Arizona, Florida or Mexico for inexpensive RV living. Small-town safety and neighbors would protect our valuables while we were on the road.

Granted, this Washington town isn't representative of the normal, everyday real estate market. But, dedicated bargain hunters can find similar conditions in many parts of the country. A factory goes bankrupt and workers follow jobs elsewhere. Logging and fishing industries fall into doldrums. A military base closes its barracks and destroys the local economy. Any number of business-related disasters can turn a wonderful residential community into a nightmare for workers. Yet, this disaster can be a windfall for those who don't have to work. Later in the book, we'll talk about how to locate these bargains.

Mind you, finding depressed towns is just one solution for low-cost retirement. If we all crowded into these places, costs would rise until they would no longer be bargains. Furthermore, too many depressed towns are depressed simply because they are boring places to live! Because you can buy a house for $20,000 does not guarantee you will enjoy living there. If the most exciting thing to do is sit on your front porch rocker and swat flies, you might as well enter a rest home.

Senior Boomers and Social Security

You hear a lot about the "Baby Boomer" generation, that titanic wave of children born right after the end of World War II and during the following decade. This boom triggered a tremendous expansion of home building, school construction and other activities designed to keep up with the growing number of children. An enormous amount of our tax dollars went to raise and educate this generation. They were the ones who used to say, "Don't trust anyone over 30!" Remember? Well, that was 25 years ago. Today, these Baby Boomers are middle aged and heading for retirement themselves. They are graying or balding, with sagging bellies. Welcome to old age, kids. Don't trust anyone over 30, indeed!

Curiously, the Baby Boomer generation opted not to have so many children. The birth rate declined—to one of the lowest points in our history. The result: the number of children has been shrinking while the number of elderly is on the rise.

One reason for so many more retirees is we are living longer. In 1900, the average length of a woman's life was 48 years; today it's almost 82 years. Men traditionally die earlier, so their lifespan is closer to 75 years. Of course, you realize that "lifespan" averages in all those who die in childhood, adolescence and middle age. It doesn't mean all men will probably die at age 75! If you arrive at age 75 in good health, you could easily expect another 15 years' life expectancy. In fact, the fastest growing segment of the population is that group of mature adults over 85!

Since we are living longer than ever before, and since the Baby Boomers are nearing retirement age, this country is now threatened with a Senior Boomer generation! Demographers estimate that before long, those over 65 years of age will outnumber teenagers by a two-to-one margin.

A problem arises when you consider that although our taxes and Social Security payments supported our retired parents and grandparents when we were working, there are now fewer taxpayers in the younger generation to support us! When the Baby Boomers join today's Senior Boomers in our golden years of retirement, our grandkids are going to have one hell of a time covering their share of Social Security, Medicare and other senior citizen programs. At that point maybe the younger generation will be saying, "Don't trust anyone over 65!"

Therefore, it just makes good sense to do some planning, to decide how we retirees are going to cope with the future. If we could get Congress to stop tinkering with Social Security funds, using them to support multi-billion-dollar boondoggles, we'd have a chance. According to New York Senator Moynihan, the government siphons over $5 billion a year from Social Security income and diverts the money to disguise budget deficits. Oh yes, they're putting paper IOUs into the drawer, planning on paying them back with deflated dollars way down the line. In the meantime, our $5 billion is not being used for the purpose intended.

Of course, all you can do about government neglect is to voice your opinion and vote. So you need to carefully look at all alternatives for retirement—no matter how much income you will have. If you approach the problem positively and sensibly, you'll find that retirement is something to look forward to, rather than dread.

Poverty and the Cost of Living

Again, as we studied retirement lifestyles and economic conditions in various sections of the country, we were impressed by wide differences in the cost of living. Some couples reported they couldn't make it on less than $20,000 a year, while others do okay on incomes of $12,000 a year.

Unfortunately, millions of folks in the United States would consider a $12,000 income a blessing. Folks who have to take minimum wage jobs find it even tougher, with incomes below $10,000 a year, less than $200 a week.

Do you earn over $6,729 a year as a single person? Then congratulations, according to the U.S. government, you are not poor! If you're married, your income must be less than $7,905 to be considered poor. That's about $129 a week for a single person and $152 for a couple. If you earn more than that, your congressmen will nonchalantly tell you that you are too affluent to be entitled to many federal programs aimed at helping the country's poor. How the government arrives at this figure is difficult to understand, yet $6,729 a year is what the fat cats figure is an adequate income for an ordinary citizen to live on. That's only $561 a month! I'd be willing to bet that the average congressman spends more than $561 each month for payments on his Mercedes-Benz. But since congressmen pay nothing for top-notch health care, most can afford two Mercedes. Yet, any income over $561 is above the poverty line!

Even worse, some politicos complain that today's retirement generation is too affluent! They feel that too much is being spent on the elderly, at the expense of the country's youth. They want to cut Medicare benefits and slash Social Security payments at the same time they increase their own salaries and medical benefits. By the government's own statistics, over three and a half million senior citizens are living below the poverty line. In 1993, the latest year for which figures are available, an additional 200,000 persons over 65 slipped below the poverty line, the highest level in 21 years. The total number of citizens over the age of 65 living in poverty has now reached four million! An additional four and a half million live on incomes of less than $10,000 a year.

Women over 65 have double the poverty rate of men of the same age; more than 15 percent fall into this category. Because women's wages are traditionally less than men's, women's Social Security payments are also low—disgracefully low. Elderly poverty is highest among single black women over 75 (40 percent of them were poor), compared with Hispanic women at 32 percent and white women at 18 percent.

This book isn't just for those who need to survive on minimal budgets. Many readers will probably enjoy perfectly adequate incomes, but they'd rather not spend it all on basic living expenses. Cutting back on one area of the budget will release funds for some luxury or a treat. Putting money aside for emergencies is a prudent move. Therefore, knowing it's possible to live on a less than average income is a reassuring thought; whether it is necessary or not, you'll always have that "ace in the hole."

Other readers, while they may own property worth a small fortune, don't feel particularly rich. Owning a home doesn't do a thing toward boosting income. Home ownership usually absorbs money from the homeowner's monthly income. After paying taxes, maintenance and miscellaneous costs of home ownership, some folks are lucky to have enough left over to buy groceries—even though their home is worth hundreds of thousands of dollars.

Despite complaints that things are going downhill for the elderly, things are not likely to change for the better. In fact, we must face the fact that the trend will continue—at least through the next decade. That is what this book is all about: facing facts and planning to live with them.

Chapter Two

Retirement Strategies

How do folks manage to retire on Social Security or its equivalent? Unless you're already accustomed to living on a limited income, it's going to take some adjusting. Not only adjusting financially, but mentally as well. The old notion of "keeping up with the Joneses" needs to be set aside. Instead of feeling depressed because your neighbors buy a new Buick every other year, you need to feel proud that you don't waste money on frills and that your old Plymouth takes you just as many places, perhaps more, because you can afford to keep gasoline in the tank.

Most folks who plan on retiring on a "shoestring" budget already know most of the ordinary tricks of saving money and economizing. You probably know all of the maneuvers and could teach me a few. But there's only so much you can save on many common expenses—items like clothing, automobiles, and so forth—since prices don't vary significantly between one store and another. Prices aren't surprisingly different between cities and states, either; many commodities are sold through national chain stores, so retail prices are similar anywhere you go. Gasoline prices do vary, of course, depending on state and local taxes, and grocery costs can be lower in some communities—depending upon competition from chain stores and availability of local produce.

There are, however, several monthly expenses which can be cut dramatically and can help stretch your budget. The most important strategy for low-cost retirement is to take control of the two most expensive budget variables: housing and utilities.

Cutting Housing Costs

Your largest savings potential lies in finding creative ways of keeping a roof over your head. This is typically the largest single outlay in anybody's budget. You have a number of cost-cutting options available to you that don't involve moving away from your home town: low-cost rentals, government subsidies and alternative housing strategies can reduce your outlays dramatically. However, in some cases—when you live in a particularly high-cost, cold-weather climate—your most dramatic savings do involve moving to a warmer climate where real estate sells for a fraction of what you're used to and where cold weather heating costs don't gobble up your spare cash.

If you're willing to move to a low-cost area, your house payments or rents will drop accordingly. Home prices vary widely around the country, in part because construction wages also vary widely. The bottom line: real estate prices and rentals are based on supply and demand. Therefore, when local wages are low, you can be sure housing costs will be moderate, otherwise residents couldn't afford to buy. A house that sells for $275,000 in one part of California can be duplicated in another part of the state for $125,000, or in Georgia for $65,000. Apartments that rent for $900 a month in one city can have counterparts in equally nice neighborhoods in smaller towns for $250, a potential savings of $650 a month.

Trimming Utility Bills

Utility rates, the second big savings potential, also differ from place to place—up to 20 percent lower in some communities. But the biggest energy hog is weather. Your electric and heating-fuel expenditures can dwarf your grocery bills when you stave off cold weather with an energy-gobbling furnace half the year, and then fight stifling temperatures with an air conditioner during the other half. Bills of $250 a month for heating and $175 a month for air conditioning are common in many locations. By moving to a section of the country where you can live without air conditioning you'll cut utility bills by a third. If you go somewhere where you need neither furnace nor air conditioner, you'll save at least another third. We've interviewed folks who cut their average utility bills from $190 a month to $40 simply by moving to a mild climate.

Adding your utility savings of $150 a month to potential housing savings of $650 (a total of $800), you've saved more than the total Social Security check for millions of retirees. When you cut expenses this drastically, you are well on your way to living "on a shoestring."

If you choose to stay put in your home town—as the majority of retirees do—there are ways of cutting utilities without pulling up stakes, leaving the kids and grandchildren. Everybody can't move to a mild climate to avoid high heating bills in the winter, and most people don't want to. Fortunately, assistance programs are out there to help low-income homeowners and renters cut energy costs. A federal effort you should know about is the Home Energy Assistance Program (HEAP), which comes to the rescue of low-income people who face unaffordable energy bills.

Although HEAP limits this assistance to heating expenses in some states, other states help with lighting and cooking costs as well. As a renter, if heating is included in the rent payments, you may be still be eligible for reimbursement. The more liberal states allow HEAP funds to pay for maintenance and repair of heating equipment, and they sometimes pay for weatherizing your home or apartment. In many areas, your local utility company gets into the act, helping you maximize your energy efficiency through weather stripping and insulating water heaters as a free service.

To qualify for HEAP, you file an application with your local department of social services or public welfare. Also, you should be prepared to prove that you are truly needy. This will be no problem if you already qualify for food stamps, receive welfare or Supplemental Security Income (SSI). But do apply as early in the year as permitted, since the federal funds for HEAP are limited; once they've been allocated, no more help is available. For information about HEAP, contact your local office of public welfare or social services department.

While you are at it, enquire about energy and utility company discounts for low-income families; it's worthwhile to check this out. Put your bid in early in the year; there's often a limit on the amount of relief available. If you use oil for heating, ask whether there's an oil buyer's cooperative in your area. Many residents band together to cut fuel costs through group purchasing power.

Recognizing that cold weather hits the low-income family hardest, many utility companies join with state and local governments to conduct energy audits and weatherization assistance. Experts will survey your home, at no charge, and show you how to save money on heating bills. Low-interest or interest-free loans are then available for you to follow through with recommendations—things like adding insulation to critical parts of the house and weatherizing doors and windows.

Eligibility rules and the scope of help vary from locality to locality, but generally preference is given homeowners or renters with homes built before a certain year. Eligibility for the audit and weatherization programs usually doesn't depend on income. To find out about programs in your area, call your state public service commission or contact: Department of Energy, Division of Weatherization Assistance, 1000 Independence Avenue, S.W., Washington, DC 20585; (202) 586-2207.

Real Estate Tax Squeeze

A third item, real estate taxes, can be tremendously important for those who insist on home ownership, yet want to live on a budget. Each state has its own unique tax structure, and each county, township and city adds its own assessments to create a bewildering patchwork of rates throughout the nation. Choosing the right tax niche is where you can save enough to make your car payments or enjoy a vacation in Hawaii every winter.

Recently, I interviewed a couple who retired from their jobs in Ohio and decided to move to Alabama. They selected a small rural community on a lake in the hill country. "This house has exactly the same square footage as our home in Ohio," the husband said, "But here we have five wooded acres with our own boat dock. We sold our old place for enough to pay cash for this home and sock a bundle in the bank." His wife added, "That's not all. In Ohio, we paid $3,600 yearly in property taxes. Here, it's $155!"

The difference between paying $300 a month in taxes and $13 a month saves enough to buy groceries and pay the utilities to boot. Taxes on a $100,000 home in Alabama average $300. No, that's not per quarter, that's per year! Alabama is not alone in having low real estate taxes. Now, when you add $300 a month in tax savings, $150 a month in utilities and housing savings of $650, you have $1,100 more in your pockets each month.

Below is a list of some of the more popular retirement states, with a ranking from lowest to highest of property tax rates. I must caution you not to take this ranking as absolute. Property taxes are so variable, depending on so many individual conditions and changing so much between communities even in the same county, that it's impossible to quote taxes state by state. Your assessments will vary depending on whether: 1) you are a veteran, 2) you have a low income, 3) you are over 65 and/or disabled, 4) your house is undervalued or overvalued, 5) your community has unusual bond debts, or 6) your county assessor is insane and/or holds a grudge against you. Another consideration is the overall tax structure, that is, when a state has no sales tax or an unusually low gasoline tax, property taxes will naturally be higher. (The state will get its money somehow.)

1. ALABAMA	8. KENTUCKY	15. OREGON
2. NEW MEXICO	9. MISSOURI	16. FLORIDA
3. MISSISSIPPI	10. NEVADA	17. WASHINGTON
4. OKLAHOMA	11. LOUISIANA	18. TENNESSEE
5. UTAH	12. N. CAROLINA	19. TEXAS
6. ARIZONA	13. VIRGINIA	20. S. CAROLINA
7. COLORADO	14. CALIFORNIA	

Medical Costs

The fourth significant cost item that varies from one part of the country to another is medical care.

Of course, doctors and hospitals are expensive everywhere, but in some areas—notably larger cities—medical costs are out of control. In my home town, an inexpensive hospital charges $1,000 a day, just for the room. Aspirins cost several dollars each. I'm not kidding—this is our economy hospital. The more expensive ones charge $2,000 a day. How many days can you afford at these rates?

Even if you have Medicare, the cost of getting sick should also fit into your formula for retiring on a shoestring. With continuing medical problems and little or no insurance, a careful investigation of hospital room costs and office-visit charges is crucial.

Another facet of the medical problem that doesn't directly involve cost is the availability of doctors. We've been told that in some areas, doctors refuse to accept new patients. To complicate the problem, some doctors and hospitals won't accept "assignments" of Medicare or Medicaid patients, except for emergency treatment. The law requires every doctor to submit Medicare claims on behalf of a patient, but they can charge more than Medicare-approved fees. You'll be stuck for the excess. This is something worth investigating if you decide to relocate when retiring.

Move Away from Your Home?

Does all this mean you must move to a low-cost area for inexpensive retirement? To another city? To another state? Not always, even though many folks find moving is the best course of action. They realize that their choice of places to live has largely been determined by their jobs. Now that they no longer have to work, they can measure the advantages of living somewhere else with a different yardstick. They are free to live anywhere they please. They can consider living in Florida, Arizona or Oregon, or anywhere.

However, for many folks, moving away is impractical. The reasons can range from not wanting to leave the grand-kids to a refusal to pull up roots after all these years. So, if you absolutely cannot picture yourselves living elsewhere, look for alternative strategies in your own community.

The first thing to do is scrutinize your present housing situation. You may be surprised to find there could be ways to dramatically cut your present housing, utility and tax expenditures without leaving your home town. This, of course, involves changing your housing situation by sell-ing your home or moving to a creative housing alternative.

Sacred Home Ownership

Let's examine some common beliefs about home owner-ship and see if they're still valid on your retirement agen-da. Most readers who will be retiring in the late '90s entered adulthood during an era of cheap and abundant real estate. Buying a house was easy. In the years after World War II—up until the '70s, when inflation pushed real estate prices past the clouds—anyone with a few hundred dollars in savings could buy a home. Monthly payments were less than rent. For the first time in history, home own-ership became so common that it was taken for granted. Our generation grew up with the conviction that it didn't make sense not to own your own home. I recall that I bought my first home in 1958 for $850 down, including closing costs. The price was $14,000 with payments of around $100 a month. A similar house would rent for about $125 a month. The deal was irresistible. Home ownership was doubly important during our working years, since interest and property taxes were deductible, thus reducing our income taxes.

In the 1950s, one man's salary could support a family, send the kids to college and maintain a comfortable subur-ban, two-car lifestyle. Most wives didn't have to work; they stayed home to take care of the house and the kids. A visit to the doctor was $10, and adequate health insurance cost $20 a month. The United States made the best cars, television sets and sewing machines money could buy, and we enjoyed the highest living standard in the entire world. Those were the good old days everyone talks about.

You don't need to be reminded that times have changed. Today, we buy our autos, sewing machines and TVs from foreign countries. College tuition is so high that both children and parents must borrow heavily to get a quality education. Today, young married couples take it for granted that both will work until retirement. What ever happened to the "Ozzie and Harriet" scenario of the wife being the homemaker while the husband earns the daily bread? Today, unless their parents can dredge up the down payment, young adults will be renting for the rest of their lives. Even if they manage the down, both will have to work full time in order to make the monthly payments, which today are usually far higher than rent on a similar place.

This decline has come gradually, with little fanfare. Many of us of who bought homes in the '50s or '60s take it for granted that property appreciation will continue on and on to infinity. Maybe it will, although the way the market has been behaving the past couple of years leads me to believe that we've reached a long-term plateau. (My guess is as good as anybody's, even though frequently wrong.) The puzzling thing is: who is going to buy these houses once the older generation is ready to begin selling them off? An entire generation could be shut out of the market unless prices drop drastically.

In any event, many retirement-age people cling to the conviction that owning a home is essential for stability and safety. They would rather cut back on their budget drastically than lose the feeling of permanence and security that home ownership provides. This is fine for those who can afford to live where they are upon retirement, those who have enough income that their lifestyles won't change appreciably when they no longer have weekly paychecks. Still others, even though they may be strapped somewhat, feel that staying in their home is worth it. After all, the grandkids live nearby, many of their neighbors are close friends, and they simply like living where they are.

However, you may find it interesting to examine your attitudes toward home ownership and see if alternatives might be worth exploring.

Costs of Home Ownership

I have a friend who is nearing retirement, and although he'll have a small monthly income, he's confident that he will make out okay. "After all, my house is paid for now, and I'll live rent-free," he explains. "I may have to pinch pennies from time to time, that's true, but at least I'll always have a roof over my head."

We talked about his financial situation, which did look somewhat flat. The company he worked for offered neither pension nor retirement plan. My friend had little in savings, having put most of his extra money into paying off the house. But on paper, he was fairly well off. After all, his California home had appreciated over the years and was now worth almost $250,000. (In other areas of the country, a comparable house might sell for as little as $75,000.)

With the paid-for house plus a few stock investments and IRAs, my friend's net worth was well over a quarter of a million bucks. Mostly on paper, of course. His Social Security income was going to be around $12,000 a year, or $1,000 a month. Yes, he and his wife could get by—just barely. But my question is why on earth should anyone worth a quarter of a million dollars have to do without well-earned luxuries?

When I suggested that he might sell the house, put the money into a safe investment and live off the interest, he was shocked. To him, that was totally irresponsible. After all, a paid-for house is a ticket to security, isn't it? "But, I'll live rent-free," he reiterated. "I'd have to pay at least a thousand a month to rent a place like this. That's my entire Social Security check!"

Try as I might, I couldn't convince him that he wouldn't be living "rent-free." The fact is, the cost of living in a paid-for home is equal to the income lost by not having the home's equity invested in high-grade securities.

Look at it this way: a business considers its store, office or factory as a capital investment; your home is exactly the same type of investment. For example, in my friend's case the after-taxes net on his home would be over $200,000 (figuring his one-time, $125,000 exemption). Even in the current fluctuating market, it was possible to find safe investments paying at least 7.5 percent—utility stocks or government-guaranteed "Ginnie Maes," for instance. Although utilities have dropped lately, these investments have been traditionally solid and safe. At 7.5 percent (what GNMAs are currently paying) my friend's house would return about $1,040 a month after taxes.

Looking at it that way, the actual cost of living in his own home is $1,040 a month ($12,500 a year) plus taxes, insurance and upkeep which add at least another $2,000 a year. Suppose he were to sell his home, invest the proceeds, then rent his neighbor's place for $900 a month—allowing the landlord to pay taxes, insurance and repairs. He would be ahead $1,680 a year. Plus, instead of forking over $2,000 yearly for real estate taxes, insurance and upkeep, he could use that money for travel or upgrading his automobile. Finally, he would have an additional $200,000 in tangible wealth, quickly available in cash.

This case may seem somewhat extreme, since few readers of this book have $250,000 homes, and since most parts of the country haven't experienced California's insane, runaway real estate prices. In order for this strategy to work there should be a wide difference between local market values and national values. Making a decision to pull down equity is not easy, and it shouldn't be made until all factors are considered and you take a deep look into that old crystal ball.

Don't misunderstand; I'm not urging everyone to sell their homes when they retire. For many that would be a terrible mistake. Several advantages come with owning property. For one thing, property ownership is usually a hedge against inflation. Should the economy go into an inflationary spiral, property probably will go up. Another benefit is that you can "homestead" your residence in the event of a lawsuit or personal bankruptcy. An alternative ploy, if you are overloaded with equity to the point of being "house poor," is to consider a "reverse mortgage."

Why Not Rent?

If, after analyzing your situation, you find you would be better off using your home equity as a cash investment, you might consider the implications of renting versus owning a home. One benefit of renting is that the landlord is responsible for repairing that leaky roof and fixing tornado damage, not you or your spouse. (A disadvantage is that if you have a cheapskate landlord, he will do none of the above.) Another happy thought is the knowledge that you don't have to live there. When your lease is up, you are perfectly free to look for a better place. Since you aren't tied to a particular locality, you can go someplace where rents are cheaper. For example: an apartment that rents for $225 a month in Daytona Beach or Austin couldn't be duplicated in Chicago for less than $650 a month. Strange as it might seem, some folks would actually rather live in Texas or Florida than in Illinois.

What are the disadvantages in renting? For someone who's always owned a home, there's a vague feeling of insecurity. If you're renting a house, you never know if the owner is going to put it on the market and you'll have to move. When you were young, moving was no big deal, but as you grow older, the chore looms larger and more distasteful. The bottom line is undeniable: you lose that sense of security that comes with home ownership.

Another disadvantage I often hear is: "It's like pouring money down a rathole. No tax breaks." Maybe there was a time in your life when that was true, when you were earning good wages and when those high property taxes and interest payments brought you a tidy income tax refund at the end of the year. And, during the time when housing was appreciating at a high yearly rate, and when capital gains were taxed at a maximum of 20 percent, you had a point. But today the situation is different. Since your retirement income will probably be low (and your Social Security nontaxable), you'll have little income to shelter with tax breaks from home ownership. Most real estate markets have cooled down, with some financial experts predicting an end to the steady appreciation of the past. The so-called tax "reform" laws stripped away some advantages of property ownership, and it's possible that even worse laws are yet to come.

No, home ownership isn't necessarily the best retirement strategy! Let's take the case of some friends of ours, a couple who had been paying $720 a month rent for an apartment—a luxury complex with a swimming pool, tennis courts and an exercise room, plus organized activities in the clubhouse. They decided to buy a home in a new development. The price was $145,000. Because of their age, the lender required $33,000 down. Their payments came to $1,148 a month, including taxes and insurance (for a 20-year loan with a low 8.75 percent interest rate). This meant an extra $428 a month added to their outgoing funds.

"Well, with the taxes and interest on the loan," they told me, "we'll get a tax break. With the apartment rent, we got nothing back at the end of the year. Renting is like pouring money down a rathole." Is it? They had to sell most of their stocks to make the down payment, stocks which paid $230 a month in dividends. If you add the loss of income to the payments, we find that it costs $1,378 a month to live in a place not much larger than their apartment—$658 more every month.

Suddenly, they found that they had to budget carefully to make the payments; they had to forgo some luxuries. They cut down on ski trips, dining out, impulse buying and other extras they'd become accustomed to before they had to pay out that extra $658 a month. Did they benefit? Yes, because of interest and property taxes, they paid no income tax that year. But since their retirement income was minimal, much of it tax-exempt, their savings were far from spectacular.

A few years ago, when real estate was continually rising in value, it wouldn't be unreasonable to expect the resale value of the home to increase by five to ten percent in a year, but this just wasn't happening in that particular market. One year later, neighboring homes were still selling at the same price. Yet, even if the home had increased in value, it wasn't money they could spend until they actually sold the place and went back to renting—where they were in the first place. The same thing applies to the equity from paying down the loan. Until they finally sell, the equity is all imaginary, on paper. No matter how you figure it, had they stayed in an apartment, they would have had an extra $7,896 in their pockets to spend that year. Some day, when property begins to appreciate and when they have their loan paid down, perhaps they can sell and turn a tidy profit. In the meantime, they are spending their retirement years investing in the future. They do, however, have the security of living in their own home, and for some folks that's very important.

Home ownership, even though the payments are high, clearly makes sense for a young couple whose earning power will probably grow over the years. As time goes by, they pay off the loan with larger paychecks, with dollars that will probably shrink from inflation. They are building for the future, just as you did at their age. But before you enter an expensive, long-term commitment to build for the future, you might want to consider whether it wouldn't be better to invest your money in your retirement rather than in some nebulous future 30 years down the line. Will you be able to enjoy your money as much 30 years from now as you can today? How old will you be then? In short, don't automatically fall for the "down the rathole" line. Figure out the financial advantages for yourself realistically, with an eye on today, not 30 years in the future.

Reasonable Rents

When working on the original edition of Retirement on a Shoestring, we mailed questionnaires to retirees in all parts of the country inquiring about housing and other living costs in their areas. When we examined several hundred responses, our figures differed significantly from the widely published cost-of-living charts. This is probably because the usual surveys average in all incomes and expenditures, including families with exceptionally high monthly incomes. Our questionnaires, however, targeted lower-income, retired folks, people who know how to economize and get along on very little. Their comments were very enlightening.

For example, some reported that two-bedroom apartments in their small towns rented for $350 or $400 a month, while two-bedroom houses rented for only $250. These figures ran counter to our expectations: houses should rent for more than apartments. We solved this puzzle when we found that in many towns the major building emphasis in recent years has been on luxury apartments. Landlords can ask top rent for a place with a swimming pool. Since older homes are in less demand, rents drop accordingly. The second factor is that our questionnaires were filled out by people on tight budgets, who wouldn't be interested in Yuppie-type houses or apartments. Therefore, they reported lower grocery budgets and tax bills as well as housing and utility costs.

Rental Assistance

There's a rental assistance program available, for those over 62 years of age or disabled, that will pay part of your rent directly to your landlord. If your income and assets fall within the limits set by the federal government you may be eligible to participate. The program is known as "Section 8 Housing" and is administered by the Federal Department of Housing and Urban Development (HUD).

In addition to qualifying financially, you have to find a landlord who is willing to participate in the Section 8 program, and the rent must fall within the limits set by the federal government. The landlord gets assurance that HUD will take care of unusual wear and tear of the property and guarantee the rent should the renter skip out. Renters get the security of never having to pay more than 30 percent of their income for rent. Check the phone book for your local housing authority office to see how long the Section 8 waiting list is. In some areas, it can be quite long.

Another rental assistance approach is the Housing Voucher program, under which a low-income elderly tenant is given a coupon that's worth the difference between 30 percent of the tenant's income and the market rental value of the apartment. The landlord doesn't have to agree to the Section 8 Housing program to participate in the Housing Voucher program. This plan is also administered by your local housing authority.

Luxury Apartments at Bargain Prices

An interesting development came out of the wild-west financial rodeo put on by Savings and Loan cowboys in the 1980s. They were responsible for building an abundance of luxury apartment complexes throughout popular retirement areas. With S&L money flowing freely, promoters and contractors raced full speed ahead to build apartment complexes before the money ran out. It didn't seem to matter that there were already too many apartments in an area. The idea was to borrow money, build, make a profit and move on to the next project. Let the government worry about cleaning up after them.

The Savings and Loan cowboys claim that their institutions "lost" billions of dollars—as if big stacks of the dollars were misplaced on the way to the store. The truth is, the money wasn't lost at all, it's simply been transferred to other people's pockets while apartment complexes and office buildings have been transferred to bankruptcy court. The bad news is that taxpayers will pick up the final bill for all of this, but the good news is that these complexes make wonderfully affordable retirement havens.

Throughout the South, particularly in Florida and Texas, renters have a wide choice of apartments with rents that often start at $300 a month. We looked at one complex in Austin, Texas, where efficiencies rented for $275 and one-bedrooms at $350 a month. This was one of the larger places, which featured two swimming pools, tennis courts, putting greens, exercise rooms and hiking paths. Because of this competition, older apartment complexes frequently offer one-bedroom apartments for as little as $250 a month. Of course, there's no guarantee that rents will stay low forever.

Near Daytona Beach, Florida, we saw a two-bedroom apartment with air conditioning, two swimming pools, lighted tennis courts and 24-hour emergency service—renting for $450. A one-bedroom place rented for $335. One retired couple explained, "We had looked at a lovely house for $80,000 and almost bought it before deciding to rent an apartment here. That $80,000 in income stocks brings in $466 a month. Our rent is only $450, so we live rent-free."

Throughout the areas where apartments are in oversupply, you'll find free, full-color booklets and brochures listing the larger apartment complexes complete with color photos of the grounds and facilities. Almost any shopping center will have these booklets, along with real estate catalogs, which also make interesting reading for those interested in buying rather than renting. The places described are fairly new and well-appointed. Older units will of course be much less.

Inexpensive Home Ownership

Some people absolutely cannot bear the thought of retiring without owning their own home. A castle that belongs to them alone, even though a small castle, is more than a luxury; it's a necessity. Having to sell the home they've lived in for years would be too much of a hardship, unless they could replace the home with a less-expensive place of similar quality. In most cases, this will require a move to another part of the country—a place where prices haven't kept pace with the galloping inflation of the '70s and '80s.

Discovering inexpensive housing is particularly exciting for us Californians who live in an area where costs have soared out of reason. Our mindset is such that we think any house costing less than $200,000 probably has something terribly wrong with its neighborhood, or lacks some amenity, such as wall-to-wall floors. When we traveled through the Sunbelt states, places like Louisiana, Georgia or the Carolinas, we were continually astonished to find nice homes selling for as low as $45,000—places which we would find very comfortable.

While traveling about Florida, checking real estate for my book *Where to Retire*, we drove past an elegant golf course development, with homes arranged near the tees so residents could play golf practically from their backyard. We weren't going to stop, because these homes seemed so far out of our financial scope that it would obviously be a waste of time. But, just to see how the rich folks live, we paused to take a look.

The homes sat on huge lots, with lovely trees and landscaping. Each house had a built-in, covered lanai, individual bathrooms for each bedroom, plus a common bath off the kitchen. Even the smallest house seemed huge, the design making it seem much larger than its two bedrooms and 1,800 square feet. Should this house be in a similar California location, the price could easily top $500,000. The Florida price: $80,000, with the contractor willing to bargain from there.

However, while an $80,000 price tag seems like a steal to our way of thinking, we realize that even that is out of reach for many retired folks. But in the same part of Florida, we looked at many homes (not on the golf course) which were selling for little more than half the $80,000 figure. In addition, we were favorably impressed by the great values and convenience in mobile home living.

Before I leave you with an impression that California is an impossible place to retire on a shoestring, let me assure you that some areas in that state offer a cost of living as inexpensive as just about anywhere you might wish to retire. The "Motherlode" country is a good example. That picturesque and historic area where gold was discovered back in the days of the '49ers is now being rediscovered by modern-day retirees. Property here is inexpensive, the climate is mild and the Sierra foothill country is great for outdoor recreation. In many areas, a house on a large, wooded parcel can be found for $50,000, whereas a smaller home on a narrow lot in one of California's high-price neighborhoods would cost $250,000. And on the ocean, in places like Eureka—where it never freezes and never gets hot—housing prices are as low as we've seen anywhere.

Best Real Estate Buys

If you plan on moving to a new community when you retire, and if you must own a house, the best strategy is to think small-town. Land, away from the bustle and economic grind of a city, is always less expensive. Because of depressed labor costs and low demand, buying a home in a small community can save you as much as 60 percent over a similar house in some metropolitan areas.

The well-known advantages of small-town living are low crime rates, the affordable cost of living and the absence of congestion. The downside is a lack of good restaurants, stores, convenient public transportation and access to medical care.

As a general rule, homes in the Southern states, the Ozarks and the Appalachian areas are excellent buys. Real estate is often bargain-priced around military bases. This is partly due to a gradual military cutback, with early retirement incentives thinning the ranks.

Wherever you find S&L money spent on apartments, you'll also find overbuilding of subdivisions and tract developments. An oversupply of houses naturally depresses the asking prices of homes. A good example of this is the Denver area, where a weekly 16-page listing of houses for sale by the government kept the market depressed for a long time. Denver's market has recovered to a great extent, but is still favorable compared with some other large cities.

It isn't only S&L problems that bring real estate bargains to the surface. Any number of factors coming together at one time can seriously depress the market. A perfect example of this is Bisbee, Arizona. This is a small mining town, with old brick Victorian buildings in a picturesque canyon setting. The town's prosperity came to an abrupt halt when the Phelps-Dodge Corporation decided to close down the mines. Without employment, families began leaving Bisbee, selling their homes when they could, abandoning them when they could not. At one point you could buy a furnished home for $4,000 or less. Some changed hands for as little as $500.

Naturally when the news got out, retirees began taking advantage of these bargains. Today, Bisbee is regaining its prosperity because of this influx of retirement money. Ajo, Arizona, also a mining town, underwent the same experience. Almost overnight, 600 houses went on the market! In a town of 3,500 inhabitants, you can imagine what this would do to prices. Again, the bonanza days are gone, but bargains still abound.

These kinds of giveaway prices don't last forever; they gradually move upward to a more sensible level. But bargains pop up any time a local economy collapses. Future bargains will predictably occur any time the government closes a military base or cancels a multi-billion-dollar defense contract. For inexpensive housing, keep your eye on news stories, and look for newly depressed areas.

Prices also drop when one or more industries fall into hard times and suspend operations. An example of this is Aberdeen, Washington. Here is a town that depended upon fishing and lumber for its livelihood. Both occupations paid good money and the area prospered. Then foreign boats, with their 30-mile-long dragnets began cleaning out the fish. Japanese factory ships started buying raw logs, processing them with low-paid Filipino workers, then selling finished lumber products to our consumers. Aberdeen's economy fluttered to a standstill. Fishing boats stayed in port. Lumber mills closed down. As people left the area, houses went on the market, but few buyers were interested.

Many towns in Washington and Oregon have been hit hard by the lumber industry's demise and most are suffering economic doldrums to one degree or another; I use Aberdeen simply as an example. In late 1994, we saw houses offered for as little as $20,000. We don't know if they were selling. We talked to a couple who had just moved there from California. They were thrilled with their home purchase. "It sits on three acres, on a hill overlooking the bay and the ocean," the husband said. "It has four bedrooms, each with its own fireplace, and a huge fireplace in the living room. It's a regular mansion, and we only paid $85,000!" In their California neighborhood, that wouldn't have bought a two-car garage.

The following are a few of the real estate bargains listed at the time of our research visit. Three-bedroom house, fenced yard, large workshop and garage area: $29,500, FHA. Two-bedroom home, completely remodeled, new appliances, new roof: $16,500. There was also a duplex listed for $14,500 and many other places listed for under $30,000. To be objective, many of these places probably sound better than they actually look, but were it not for the ailing economy, most would sell for two or three times the price. Before you start packing for Aberdeen, however, be aware that it has a cool climate, with lots of overcast days and winter rain. The upside is that like most Washington coastal towns, winters are relatively snow-free.

Sharing Housing

Still, to reduce your monthly housing outlay, it's not necessary to move away from your home town. There are several ways you can cut costs and stay around family and friends. One way is through house sharing.

In Europe, the concept of more than one family to a home is traditional, as it was in the United States in the early part of this century. During the Depression, people thought nothing of families doubling up to share expenses. A large house can easily accommodate many more people than usually live there. After World War II, a tremendous housing boom made housing readily available and cheap. It then became almost obligatory for every family to own its own little piece of real estate. Shared housing and double-family living became a thing of the past.

Today, with real estate priced out of reach for many people, the idea of house sharing is returning to the American scene. For those who are retired and who don't own a home, or for those who can no longer afford the burdens of home ownership, the notion of house sharing is especially attractive. If you own a large house, which is empty now that the children are out on their own, sharing with another retired couple is one way to cut costs and make money at the same time.

Group living turns out to be a very efficient as well as convenient way to cut living costs. This is particularly true in some of the more desirable but expensive locations. "If we were to rent a home in this neighborhood," said one couple, "we would have to pay at least $1,000 for rent and utilities. That just wasn't in the cards. We found another couple and a single lady to go in with us, and we've cut our rent expenses to about $350 a month."

How do you find these situations? The most common contact is the classified section of your daily newspaper. The number of "housemates wanted" advertisements grows in direct proportion to the increases in housing costs. There are also private and non-profit agencies that specialize in placing individuals in shared housing. Your telephone book's classified section will put you in touch with these agencies. Your local area Agency on Aging can sometimes help you locate these arrangements: call (800) 677-1116 for the nearest source of help.

Shared housing is not just for retirement-age people. Many arrangements have multi-generational "families," in which young, middle-aged and elderly live as one cooperative unit. Others are organized according to sex; women often prefer to live with other women rather than have disruptive menfolk dirtying up the house (as we men are entirely capable of doing).

Obviously, in order to make a success of one of these situations, the group's members must be compatible. This isn't the place for someone who is rigid, closed-minded or who doesn't like being around people. Making the decision to try a shared housing lifestyle requires that you not only investigate the situation very thoroughly, but also objectively analyze your own personality. Ask yourself some questions. Do noise and confusion disturb you? Would pets bother you? Would you be terribly upset if someone weren't as neat as you are? What if a living companion left underwear hanging on the shower curtain? If these things bother you, or if you are notorious for the offenses mentioned above, you should think things over carefully before making a decision. In any event, see if you can't do a trial month's stay to make sure everyone is like-minded and compatible.

Other considerations: Will the space be adequate? How much of the house will be yours besides the bedroom? Will you have room for your hobbies? How are decisions made in the house? Is it a democracy or is someone in charge—perhaps the owner or the original tenant? Neither arrangement is preferable to the other, but you ought to know how it works in advance. If the person in charge is strict but fair, and if everyone knows where the boundaries are and precisely what the responsibilities are, there should be few problems. But if that person is a tyrant, you may be better off elsewhere. On the other hand, a democratic management—with each resident politicking, lobbying and arguing heatedly over each and every excruciating detail of life in the house—can be just as bad. A happy medium is always the best path.

There should be sharing of work responsibilities, chores and perhaps cooking. Often housemates take turns cooking supper, giving the others a break. "There are ten of us living in our house," said one lady as she detailed her experiences in shared housing. "Each of us is responsible for preparing three dinners every month and for cleaning up afterward. That means that except for our three chore days, we have dinner waiting for us every night. We can watch the evening news or read a novel and relax, before and after dinner. The dinners are excellent, too, because each of us cooks our favorite meals and tries to outdo the others!"

Further questions are: Will you be close to shopping and transportation? If you have an auto, will you have a parking space? You also need to decide the kind of house partners you'd like to live with. Some groups behave like small, extended families, while others are more formal, with relationships on a neighborly rather than familial level. Note, too, that a larger group gives more of an opportunity to choose friends and to spread expenses over a larger base.

Sometimes a shared housing unit can be quite large, from 20 to 200 units operated as a commercial enterprise, and is referred to as "congregate housing." This arrangement is suitable for those in good health, but who may need assistance in everyday chores, cooking, housekeeping and shopping, or who don't want to be bothered with doing any of the above. The living quarters are small, usually with a tiny kitchen, and there is a group dining room where residents can take meals if they wish. Cooking and housecleaning are done by staff. Sometimes these units are federally subsidized and available only to low-income elderly applicants.

Intentional Community Housing

Shared housing doesn't always involve casual or informal groups getting together to share a house. There is a growing movement toward planned, or "intentional," communities. Though sometimes these are small, family-type affairs, many are larger groups, more like clubs, where people with common interests band together to forge new lifestyles and to share expenses and experiences. The intentional community differs from ordinary shared housing in that there is usually a common goal or special shared beliefs among the participants. They think of themselves as "members" rather than simply "neighbors." For a complete listing of interesting locations, look for a book in your library called Intentional Communities, A guide to Cooperative Living, published by Communities Publications Cooperative, Stelle, IL, 1991. This book may be out of print, but it's packed with information.

Ecological concerns are a prevalent theme of many intentional communities. Some of these experiments are outgrowths of communities started during the "hippie" era; others are more modern in origin. There are communities for women only, for couples, or for mixed and intergenerational members. Some communities are religiously oriented, often receiving funds from a church. You'll find all spectrums of religious beliefs represented in intentional communities, from conservative Baptists to broad-minded Unitarians, even one community with a spiritual focus which combined "feminist witchcraft" and Buddhism!

Most intentional communities are owned by members and often provide free room and board in return for a specified amount of work. Other groups demand a stipend or at least require a sharing of expenses. Some charge a monthly fee plus work requirements in exchange for residence and seminars. Residents work at chores such as kitchen and garden pursuits, teaching, housekeeping, maintenance and a variety of other jobs. Some facilities are located on farms, others in forest or desert settings, while still others are urban collectives.

Recently a friend visited several intentional communities and reported enthusiastically on two, one of which she intends to join upon retirement. The fee is $330 a month plus 20 hours a week of work, in exchange for all meals, nice living quarters and an exciting intellectual ambience. (At her request, I am withholding the name of this community because of her fears that readers might flood the place with applications before her retirement.)

Be aware that some communities are in the process of formation and may never get off the ground, so be cautious about investing time and money in a mere pipe dream. Many do not actively solicit new members, so don't think you can simply drop in and take up residence. First you need to contact the group to see if there are any openings and if your interests coincide.

One point to keep in mind: just because an organization offers inexpensive living doesn't mean you will be happy there. One community listing sounded all right, except it described its member residents as equally divided among "straight, gay/lesbian, bisexual and undecided sexual propensities." (Wait a minute: suppose I don't fit into any of the above categories, what then?) Another group, still in the process of forming, plans on building an undersea village where you will be surrounded by the "awesome beauty of the sea."

Continuing Care Retirement Communities

As the retiree population grows ever larger, there is a corresponding rise in the number of housing complexes devoted exclusively to senior citizens. An increasingly popular development in retirement communities is the concept of long-range, total care facilities.

Three conceptual stages of retirement are combined in these developments. First: houses, cottages or apartments for those who want to be totally independent and who prefer to cook for themselves. Next there are facilities for folks who aren't quite up to doing their own cooking (or are totally fed up with it) or who might have trouble taking care of themselves. These residents live in apartments, but take meals in the dining room. Finally, there is a stage where skilled nursing care and a traditional nursing home environment is provided in hospital-type rooms, if and when they become too infirm to take care of themselves.

Some of these complexes are very, very expensive. Obviously, given the exorbitant cost of medical care in this country, you can understand why. Recently we heard of one place that requires a $400,000 investment (non-refundable on death) and $2,000 a month for expenses. However, because of ever-increasing competition, we're seeing a proliferation of affordable full-service retirement homes. The least expensive place we found charged about $35,000 to enter and about $690 a month for expenses. This was in a small city on Oregon's coast. A monthly income of around $1,000 and some financial net worth are required. This is not exactly "retirement on a shoestring," but if that's the type of security you're looking for, you can find a satisfactory place with some investigation.

One couple who moved into one of these lifetime care units said, "When we retired and moved to this part of the country, our only question was whether to buy a house or to rent. This is a compromise between the two." They bought into this complex ten years earlier, both at the age of 60. At the time of the interview they were thinking of giving up their villa and moving into the second stage of the complex. "A nice thing about this arrangement is that we keep pace with our friends. The friends we know as golfing or bridge partners will be with us in the next stage. If they aren't ready to move yet, they soon will be. As we grow older and our interests change, we move along together."

Limited-Care Communities

For those who are unwilling or unable to pay the expensive entrance fees of continuing care, there is an alternative more practical for budget retirement: a retirement community without extensive health care. These are usually stand-alone facilities, that is to say, without medical care of any kind, although sometimes a nurse is on call. Although each unit—whether an efficiency, one- or two- bedroom apartment—has a full kitchen, meals are usually served in a dining room. These facilities are becoming competitive, and some bargains can be found. The major difference is that you must be able to take care of yourself without medical supervision. Depending upon where it's located, prices for these places can start as low as the mid-$600 a month range, including meals, housekeeping services and all utilities except telephone. This is an ideal arrangement for singles who don't want to bother with full housekeeping.

More than three million Americans now live this way, an increase of 300 percent over the past 15 years. A boom in new retirement housing of this type is evident throughout the country, with construction not keeping pace with demand. When you consider recent studies which show that the number of Americans over 85 years of age will top 24 million in the next half century, the need should be apparent.

Subsidized Housing

Until the 1980s, the U.S. government attempted to do something about low-cost housing through Housing and Urban Development (HUD) programs. Government money subsidized both the construction and monthly rentals for qualifying retirees. However, the outlook today is bleak indeed, with continuing cuts in the funding. The number of new affordable housing units dropped from 26,000 in the early 80s, to 9,000 in 1994, and down to an expected 1,000 in 1995. Despite a continuously growing number of poverty-line retirees, assistance shrinks.

According to the Retirement Housing Foundation, 250,000 low-income retirees are on waiting lists for low-cost retirement facilities. The odds of being accepted are about one in eight. However, should your local HUD-sponsored facility have a long wait, you might check around with other communities. As an example: Audrey W. qualified for low-cost housing, but when she applied at a popular, upscale Pacific Coast town, she was informed that it would be at least six years before her name could possibly come up for a HUD-subsidized apartment. Then she discovered a small town in a beautiful Sierra Nevada location with a waiting list of a few months. She moved there, intending to rent until something opened up, but because she could legitimately plead hardship—with an income and resources well below the allowable amount—Audrey was rewarded with a one-bedroom apartment for payments equalling 27% of her net monthly income. After deductions and allowances—according to a complicated formula—her rent came to about $50 per month.

One of the largest non-profit providers of subsidized retirement facilities, the Retirement Housing Foundation operates 124 retirement communities in 23 states. All units are HUD approved, and the tenants' rents are partly subsidized by HUD. In other, non-HUD subsidized units, residents pay a deposit and competitive rents, although these are somewhat lower than a conventional commercial facility because of the HUD low-interest mortgages.

Retirement Housing Foundation manages a total of 7,918 subsidized apartments and 3,777 non-subsidized units. These include a few assisted-living and skilled-nursing units. For information, contact: Retirement Housing Foundation, 5150 E. Pacific Coast Hwy, #600, Long Beach, CA 90804; (310) 597-5541, ext. 162. The other large provider is: National Church Residences, 2335 Northbank, Columbus, OH 43220; (614) 451-2151.

Investigate Before Moving In!

In any kind of shared or cooperative living, certain conditions must be thoroughly understood. Ideally there will be a contract, especially if you will be renting from a private or public entity rather than just informal sharing. If you are going to have to put up any money, here are some things you need to know.

How much, if any, of the entrance fee is refundable? Are there additional expenses besides the monthly fees? Should you die, will your heirs receive a portion of your entrance fee or deposit? Suppose you are unable to pay the monthly fee, is there any financial assistance available? Are there any controls on how much fees can go up? Under what conditions can the arrangement be terminated by either side? Usually there's a three-month trial period, so you should have the right to cancel and get a refund of your entrance fee. Nonrefundable entrance fees should be avoided. You might want to check with the Better Business Bureau to see if there have been complaints against the facility and whether they are in good financial shape.

The American Assoc. of Homes for the Aging's publication, *The Consumer's Directory of Continuing Care Retirement Communities*, lists more than 300 retirement communities. Your library should have a copy. For info on shared housing, contact the National Shared Housing Resource Center (Burlington, VT) at (802) 862-2727, or write to AARP Fulfillment, 601 E St. NW, Washington, DC 20049. Another information source is the National Consumers League, 815 15th St. NW, #928, Washington, DC 20005; (202) 639-8140.

Chapter Three

Working and Retirement

Work begins the day we enter kindergarten. That's when our on-the-job training begins (without pay, of course). We quickly learn that we have an obligation to get up every morning—whether we want to or not—and that we must appear at a certain place at a certain time. We discover that we have a "boss" (the teacher), and we must please the boss if life is going to be tolerable. Until each long, wearisome school day draws to a merciful close, teachers and administrators direct our souls, control our lives and limit our leisure. I'm convinced that the fourth grade is the longest period of time ever measured. (Fourth grade recess being the shortest time ever measured.)

By the time we finally finish school and enter the job market, we've learned our lessons well. Get up every day, go somewhere, perform work we may or may not enjoy, and be rewarded with a weekly paycheck instead of a report card. Weekends off, plus a two-week vacation, are the only respite from the grinding schedule. To miss a day's work means losing a day's pay—a serious blow to many budgets—so we go to work even though we feel terrible. Missing too many days means losing a job—a disaster.

This process, started in kindergarten, is relentlessly reinforced through the next sixty years of our lives. We suffer from a mental hang-up called the "work ethic." To have a job is good. Not to have a job is bad. To lose a job is ruinous. Only bums live without working.

Suddenly—willingly or not—you stumble into retirement. You no longer have a job, someone to boss you, or a place to be every day at a specified hour—or else. You can get up when you please, take a nap when you please, and you don't have to please anyone who doesn't please you.

For some people, this is wonderful: the goal they've worked for and anticipated since that first day in kindergarten. School's out! Vacation from now on! When you get up in the morning, you can roll over and take a nap!

But for many, retirement is a terrible shock. There's something wicked or evil about breaking this pattern of responsibility to a job. When one of these individuals wakes up in the morning without a job to go to, a feeling of guilt sets in. "Something is terribly wrong here," the person thinks. "I should be working, suffering, making money..."

This guilty feeling is why many folks refuse to retire, even though they work at jobs they hate. Others, when forced into retirement, insist on finding full-time or part-time jobs, whether they need the money or not. To me, this seems like a tragic waste of a lifetime's goal.

Retirement shouldn't mean dropping out of the world, and it doesn't necessarily mean the end of a person's working career. On the contrary, for most folks retirement means the chance to do what they want to do rather than what they have to do. You now have the time to write a book, join an actor's group, become a fishing guide or turn your hobby into a profitable occupation. This may be the time to take up a new hobby, to explore an unlimited range of options. Learn to feel sorry for those who still have to work instead of feeling guilty for not being with them.

For those who need to be "doing something" but who can get by without extra income, we recommend volunteering. As a volunteer, you will not only be doing something meaningful and worthwhile, but you meet other volunteers, widen your network of friends and lay the groundwork for later years when you may need volunteers to help you. We'll discuss volunteer work later.

Expensive Jobs

On the other hand, many retirees desperately need extra earnings to supplement their Social Security or other pension income. Part-time or full-time jobs can mean the difference between bare survival and a comfortable retirement. Yet, sometimes the income earned can be costly—in several ways.

A condition that can make a job uneconomical is the government's attitude toward working while drawing Social Security. To discourage retirees from earning money, the government reduces benefits when you earn more than a certain amount. If you are under 65, you are permitted to earn $8,040 ($670 a month), and then you'll be penalized one dollar for every two dollars you earn over that amount. If you are over 65, you can earn $11,160 ($930 a month) before they deduct one dollar for every three you earn. Once you are over 70 years old, you can earn as much as you like.

Let's take the case of Roger, a commercial printer who lost his $14-an-hour job because desktop publishing put his employer out of business. Since he was 62 years old, Roger applied for Social Security and was entitled to $768 a month (amounting to $9,216 a year or $177 a week). Finding he needed more income, he looked for a job. The best he could find paid $6.45 an hour ($258 a week). Better than nothing, he thought. At the end of the year, he discovered that he had to repay $2,430 of his Social Security money, because at $6.45 an hour he earned too much money! For full-time employment, Roger was only entitled to make $3.86 an hour without penalty; that's less than minimum wage. In other words, Roger worked more than nine weeks for nothing—just to make up for the money deducted from his Social Security! To add insult to injury, he had to pay income taxes on the excess $2,430. He immediately started looking for a part-time job.

Good Jobs and High Prices

Part-time work is the solution for many starvation budgets. The problem is, competition for these jobs can be fierce and pay can be very low. This creates a dilemma: where part-time jobs are plentiful and pay is good, you'll find the cost-of-living impossible. A booming economy brings high rents and elevated living costs as well as high wages. It doesn't make sense to retire where living costs are exorbitant in order to find a good-paying part-time job, in order to be able to afford the extra expenses of retiring in a costly area! You're right back where you started.

I have a friend who lived in a nice apartment in Monterey, California. Her rent was $700 a month. The high cost of living in Monterey wouldn't permit her to live on Social Security. She found a part-time job in a bookstore that paid $6.00 an hour ($400 a month clear) for working five afternoons a week (20 hours). If she earned more than this, she would start losing Social Security benefits. When she decided to move to a smaller town in a lower-cost area, she found an equally nice apartment for $300 a month. Part-time jobs there paid about $4.50 an hour, but no jobs were available. At first she was disappointed—until she realized that the $400 she saved in rent made up for the $400 she had been earning at her bookstore job. In other words, she had been going to work five afternoons a week just to pay higher rent. Now she devotes her time to very satisfying volunteer work in the community.

Finding Retirement Jobs

Some retirees have lifetime job skills that make it relatively easy to find part-time work. Even though they no longer have the strength and stamina to handle some of the tougher jobs, their experience and good judgment qualify them for consulting and/or supervisory work. Perhaps you have a skill that is in demand for vacation fill-ins or emergency work in case of an employee's illness. Nurses, secretaries, bookkeepers and others with specialized work backgrounds find themselves in great demand for these temporary positions. Example: I have a brother—a retired veterinarian—who doesn't care to work on a regular basis. It turns out that many small veterinary clinics are one-doctor outfits; taking a vacation is out of the question unless another vet can fill in. This works out perfectly for my brother, who schedules the vacations well in advance and limits the number of weeks he works to those he chooses.

Of course, not everybody has high levels of competency at a trade or profession, and many skills have been replaced by computers, so it isn't always easy to find part-time work. However, just about everyone has something valuable to contribute to the job market, even if it's just enthusiasm and a willingness to work.

The Yellow Pages of your telephone directory will list temporary employment firms, such as Manpower or Kelly (used to be Kelly Girls, remember?). They nearly always need temporary or seasonal workers and can usually be depended on to find you a job when needed. These jobs have a way of becoming a regular thing when the employer is pleased with a worker's performance. The good thing about these situations is that it's understood from the beginning that they are temporary, so you aren't in an embarrassing position if you quit after you've earned as much as Social Security permits.

Another way to look for work is to inquire at the local senior citizens' center. They can direct you to a Senior Citizen Council office (if it isn't in the center itself) where the staff works at placing senior citizens in both permanent and temporary jobs. Of course, the newspaper's help-wanted classified pages carry employment opportunities, but many prefer younger applicants. By placing your own ad in the situation-wanted column, you can put forward your own unique qualifications, job requirements and preferences. If you have special skills that might be attractive to a particular group of employers, the telephone book will provide a mail list for you to send out résumés. As a final resort, there's always the state employment bureau, or human development department—whatever it calls itself in your area. There, however, you are competing with unemployed workers who are looking for jobs while collecting unemployment benefits.

The Senior Community Service Employment Program helps low-income persons, age 55 or older, find part-time work in community service through the Job Training

Partnership Act. This program provides training to individuals who are interested in working in the private sector. To find out the address and telephone number of your local agency on aging, contact the Administration on Aging's Elder Care Locator at (800) 677-1116.

The National Council on Aging and the National Council of Senior Citizens attempts to provide part-time employment opportunities for older workers in public agencies, community service agencies, libraries, hospitals and schools. Applicants must be 55 or older and low-income. Participants in the program work 20 hours a week, usually at minimum wage. For information, contact the National Council on Aging, 409 Third Street, S.W., Suite 200, Washington, DC 20024; (202) 479-1200. Or, try the National Council of Senior Citizens, 1331 F Street, N.W., Washington, DC 20004; (202) 347-8800.

Check with your local American Association of Retired Persons (AARP) organization; they often offer career counseling and support a program called "Workers' Equity Initiative." AARP has a computer database of employers who need older workers. They can also advise you of your rights under the federal Age Discrimination Act. If you are interested, you might request AARP's free publications: "How to Stay Employable: A Guide for the Mid-life and Older Worker" and "Working Options—How to Plan Your Job Search, Your Work Life. Contact AARP Fulfillment, 601 E St. NW, Washington, DC 20049.

A well-stocked bookstore will have several books on how to find jobs and how to start your own business. A mail order company called The New Careers Center, in Boulder, Colorado, has a full collection of these kinds of books. They cover subjects such as finding jobs with a cruise line or in national parks, teaching English abroad, starting a business in your own home and freelancing opportunities. Don't expect to find any astounding secrets for making money, but these books could be the source of new ideas on work opportunities. Write and ask for The Whole Work Catalog, New Careers Center, P.O. Box 339-CT, Boulder, CO 80306.

Sales Work

For the outgoing personality, one of the easiest jobs to land is commission saleswork. The reason is obvious: the employer pays no salaries or benefits until you sell something. Automobile agencies typically have half a dozen salespersons lounging about in hopes that a buyer will happen along. Real estate offices can afford to have large staffs because they don't pay wages. Often, the salesperson is obligated to spend some time each week taking care of the office (at no pay) in addition to sales work. Many sales positions offer little or nothing in the way of wages, expecting the employees to earn the bulk of their income from commissions. When successful, these jobs make good part-time occupations, and sometimes pay well. The nice part about these jobs is that you needn't invest any capital, other than a few nice clothes. The down side is when things aren't selling, you not only get nothing for your time, but it can also be boring. (Please, before you consider investing any money in a sales business, check very, very carefully; the majority of these are scams.)

The Underground Economy

The Internal Revenue Service is understandably concerned with what it calls the "underground economy." Throughout the country, folks are dealing with each other in cash transactions—or trading goods and services which amount to income—yet they neglect to report these transactions on their income tax forms.

For example: if you do housework for someone in exchange for reduced rent, you should report the rent as wage income while the landlord reports your labor as rental income. If you sell items at a flea market, you are supposed to report your profits. I don't know if it's ever happened, but that's the way it's supposed to be. Without a "paper trail" of transactions, and since individual amounts are relatively insignificant, the IRS finds it almost impossible to track these small-time tax evaders. The IRS seems genuinely surprised and indignant over these trans-gressions, and estimates that if everyone paid income tax on all their earnings there would be additional billions pouring into our national coffers every year. On the other hand, if the wealthy were limited in their loopholes, the amount of additional revenue would be staggering. But as we all know, since tax laws are written by wealthy con-gressmen, of course they tend to favor wealthy taxpayers.

Arts and Crafts

Now that you are retired, you'll have more time to spend on your favorite hobby. When your pastime involves arts and crafts, you have a potential for turning it into cash, selling your wares at local craft shows, fairs, flea markets and by consignment to gift shops. If you have a product that is unique and of high quality, you might find it accept-ed at a national craft consignment shop. The Elder Crafters is one such place: a non-profit organization that accepts handcrafted work by artists 55 years or older. Each sub-mission is reviewed by a committee before being accepted. Out-of-state consignments are common. If customers or other dealers are interested in your work, Elder Crafters will put you in touch with them. A set of color slides of your work, along with a query letter, is recommended. There's a one-time, non-refundable application fee of $5 and a $10 annual fee if you are accepted. Contact Elder Crafters at 405 Cameron Street, Alexandria, VA 22314; (703) 683-4338.

Arts and crafts shows are big business in many parts of the country, and some retirees make a good living this way. I interviewed Jean and her husband Dwan—a Clarksville, Tennessee, couple—who devote much of their spare time to their hobby-business. They travel to craft fairs in several Southern states as far away as Florida, selling all the hand-icrafts they can make.

"Our best time of the year is fall," Jean said, "from Labor Day until the first week in December. The closer to Christmas, the better the sales of lower-priced items.

Anything priced ten dollars or less sells like hotcakes."
Jean specializes in tole-painted objects: shelves, breadbox-
es, wall plaques, and other small items. "Dwan works with
the bandsaw, and I do the painting," she explained. "From
January on through to August, we build our inventory, and
then we go on the road."

Their net profit averages between $1,000 to $1,500 a
weekend, although some of the more successful sellers can
take in as much as $15,000 at one of the larger craft fairs,
where as many as 40,000 visitors browse the shows.
However, to get a booth at one of these high-volume shows
requires exceptionally good products (you need to submit
good-quality slides and samples of your work), a substantial fee for the selling space and a long time spent on the
waiting list. Jean described one show in Ann Arbor that's
reputed to have a waiting list several years long.

To locate these arts and crafts shows, pick up a copy of
Sunshine Artists USA, a magazine that bills itself as "The
Voice of the Nation's Artists and Craftsmen," listing 10,000
arts and crafts shows in the United States. Write: Sunshine
Artists USA, 1700 Sunset Dr., Longwood, FL 32750.

Free Flea-Market Enterprises

Forty years ago, when I first met my friends Jack and
Marie, they were the epitome of early-day "yuppies." Jack
had just graduated from a university with a degree in business. Marie was making money hand over fist from a direct
sales enterprise she had started. Clearly, this couple was
headed for the top. And that's exactly where they went.
Unfortunately, a few years before retirement, a series of
accidents and some bad investments seriously diminished
their financial portfolio. But not their drive to succeed.
Although far from poverty-stricken, Jack and Marie felt
they wanted to earn money and decided to use their business knowledge to do it.

"The problem was," said Marie, "we didn't have the
'seed money' necessary to get into a substantial business.
Besides, we were retired; we wanted to control our time,

and not be slaves to business hours. Since we both enjoy meeting the public and selling, we figured what could be more natural than working flea markets?"

So, for the past several years, they've been traveling to flea markets and an occasional craft fair in their van. At times, they sleep in the van to save on motel bills. They pick up merchandise to resell from auctions, distress sales and wholesalers. Garage sales sometimes provide stock., "But we stop at garage sales only if we happen to be driving past," said Jack. "Most of the time, people want more for their junk than we can get for it at the flea market!" Classified ads in the local newspaper are another source of merchandise, especially when a family is moving away and is anxious to get rid of everything.

What's required to become an entrepreneur in the flea market business? You'll need a van large enough to carry your inventory, some folding tables, a canvas awning to keep off sunshine and (God forbid) rain. And of course, you'll need to fill your van with interesting items for sale.

To find out where flea markets are, just attend one, visit a few booths and talk with the proprietors; you'll discover which locations are more lucrative and which to stay away from. Also, most state tourism offices and chambers of commerce list flea market events.

House and Pet Sitting

Remember when you used to go on vacation? You'd load the kids and the dogs into the car, lock the front door and head for the mountains. If you forgot to lock the front door, no big deal. Probably you paid a neighbor's kid 50 cents to mow the lawn while you were away.

That was before the days of mass burglaries, vandalism and "no pets allowed" signs at your favorite resort.

Times have changed. Many people now insist on a "house watcher" while they go on vacation, business trips or extended visits. Furthermore, they no longer trust the neighbor's kid to watch over things, not as long as he has access to spray-paint and a penchant for graffiti.

Vacationers are willing to pay real money to mature adults in exchange for peace of mind. It's no longer 50 cents a lawn. Today the going rate is often $10 an hour and up, and well worth it.

One lady we interviewed managed to build her pet care and home-watching business into a full-time job. She even has to hire help during the busy season. For $15 a day, she makes two trips to each home. She feeds the pets, exercises them for a few minutes if necessary; waters the house plants as needed; changes the lighting to make it appear the home is occupied; carries in newspapers and mail, and checks the telephone answering machine for important messages. Total time: two half-hour visits each day. Four customers a day constitutes a maximum schedule, for an average of $300 a week in cash. Her business grew by word of mouth, spending nothing on advertising. "I'm afraid that if I put an ad in the "yellow pages," I'd have so much business I'd never get back into retirement!"

Part-Time Teaching

Teaching is an excellent (although not always lucrative) way to take advantage of your life experience. Throughout the country, courses in trade schools and adult education classrooms are often canceled because no instructors are available. The problem can be especially critical in smaller towns where qualified craftsmen forsake the low wages paid in the community and head for the bigger cities. This means students are deprived of the opportunity of learning a trade or a skill that perhaps you could provide.

The requirement to be a teacher in this circumstance is not necessarily a college degree, it's often just a solid knowledge of your craft and the ability to pass your skills on to the students. Even in states where academic qualifications are strict for community college and trade schools, Adult Ed instructors seldom have to match the formal requirements demanded of academic instructors.

I once volunteered to work as a teacher's aide in an English-as-a-foreign-language section of the local adult education program. I enjoyed it immensely, but when I tried to quit my volunteer position, the school administrators begged me to stay. They insisted on putting me on a paid basis and granting me a lifetime California teaching credential in English as a bonus. All I really wanted to do was have fun helping foreigners learn our language.

Teaching opportunities are often advertised in the local newspaper classifieds. A phone call to the relevant school department, especially to the Adult Education office, will verify whether there are any openings. If they don't have anything available, they surely know where to refer you. Some departments will actually create a class to fit an instructor's skills. If they can locate 15 or 20 students who are interested in your specialty, the school will receive money from the state to fund the class and pay your salary. It's best to prepare a résumé, detailing your work experience and what aspects of this experience you are capable of teaching. If you have some college credits, don't fail to mention them.

Many school districts find themselves faced with a shortage of substitute teachers for regular grade school and high school classes (partly because of the low pay scales for substitutes). If you have at least a bachelors degree, many schools are eager to put you on their substitute list, even though you have no teaching credential. Classroom assistant jobs, almost always part-time, are possibilities for those with little or no experience. Starting off as a volunteer is an excellent way to break in. Private schools don't always demand approved teaching credentials, and because their regular salaries are often lower, they offer a lot of job opportunities. If you have some formal education, and feel qualified to teach a subject, you might consider a part-time position in a private school.

A real bonus is that working in a school situation puts you in contact with the community, creating an ideal situation for meeting new people and making friends. If you're a stranger in town, this is the quickest way to lose that status and become known and appreciated.

Beware of Fancy Advertisements

Magazines are liberally sprinkled with ads urging you to start your own business, and the advertiser offers to help you get started. If you've been around long enough to think about retirement, you've also got the smarts to know these things are too good to be true. The ads claim you can make $100 an hour cleaning carpets, selling stationery or some other scheme, but you end up paying lots of money for nothing. Local newspaper ads can sometimes be phony as well. I had a friend who answered an ad that offered to set up applicants with a free delivery route business, stocking supermarkets with a nationally known product. He should have known there was something wrong when the company insisted that he buy an expensive delivery van from them—at their price—and when the company "union" demanded a huge initiation fee. It turned out that the union and company were splitting the initiation fees and down payments. These "employees" were laid off when new applicants came up with enough money to buy a truck and make union initiation fees. To top it off, the company terminated the job but not the payments on the van. Oh well, he was able to use the van for camping and eventually drove his money's worth out of it.

Be aware that how-to-do-it schemes for earning lots of money at home can be overly optimistic, to say the least. Don't pin your future on a flowery magazine advertisement assuring you that you can make $100,000 a year in your spare time. One example I am familiar with is books claiming to have the secrets of making a good living by travel or other freelance writing. As a long-time freelancer, I can assure you that I would have starved long ago had I depended upon travel or feature articles for food on the table. What self-help books don't tell you is that newspapers have access to tons of travel articles and feature material from syndicated wire services—for free. Unless you have something of special interest to local readers, newspapers would be wasting money; they already have more free material than they could possibly use. The few papers that do use freelancers often have such a small budget for outside material that it's hardly worth the postage. Successful magazines usually employ staff writers, and run-of-the-mill publications often pay no better than newspapers, and sometimes not at all. They feel that a byline is sufficient reward.

That's not to say there are not rewards in freelance writing. The rewards come in the satisfaction of being published, in ego gratification and an occasional freebie from a business looking for publicity. With notable exceptions, stingy publishers and tiny paychecks place most freelancing in the category of a hobby rather than a business.

Starting Your Own Business

Before you think of starting a home business, you need to examine your own personality, to ask yourself some questions and supply some honest answers. From the book Starting a Mini-Business: A Guidebook for Seniors (by Nancy Olsen, Fair Oaks Publishing, Sunnyvale, CA, 1988) come some of the following ideas on this subject. Ask yourself these questions:

1. Are you a self-starter? If you are one of those who hate getting up in the morning and getting after business, being your own boss won't be any fun.

2. How do you feel about dealing with people? You need to like working with people if you are going to get into your own business. Almost all types of business require daily contact with others.

3. Can you take responsibility? Are you the type who can forge ahead and get things done, or have you always expected others to do things for you?

4. How good an organizer are you? Running a business means being organized. You're going to have to keep books, records, and keep your fingers on all the strings.

5. Can you make decisions? At every turn in the road, there will be instant choices to be made. If you can't, you're going to be paralyzed. Your business will suffer.

6. Can you stick with it? You can't always expect to make money from the very beginning. If you don't

encounter instant success, are you going to become discouraged before your enterprise gets the chance to fly?

7. How good is your health? Will you truly have the energy to follow through on your business?

If after analyzing yourself, you are still assured that you really want to go into business, you might check with your local office of the U.S. Small Business Administration. There are 100 offices in cities nationwide, offering free counseling, literature and sometimes financial assistance for starting a business.

RV Work Opportunities

Motorhomes and travel trailers figure importantly in many retirement lifestyles. Some folks use RVs for part-time retirement, and many live in their rigs year-round. This mobile way of living lends itself perfectly to seasonal jobs in national or state parks and private campgrounds. These positions offer free park rent and often a salary for minimal working hours. Seasonal jobs like these aren't limited to RV travelers; many parks supply conventional housing for their employees. But one of the advantages of RV travel is the ability to take your home with you to the job site. This opens many new work opportunities.

When a seasonal migration of snowbirds descend upon a popular RV area, temporary employees are in great demand at the resorts. Handymen, cooks and workers of all types usually receive free rent in addition to salary.

Almost every business in town needs extra help to handle the increased tourist traffic. From gift shops to garages, from restaurants to recycling, temporary help is needed. RV mechanics and repairmen can write their own agendas when thousands of RVs are in town.

Temporary jobs in RV parks and campgrounds can include assistant managers, clerical staff and groundskeepers. When the RVs pull out, the RV park's staff often drops back to just the manager. Ski instructors are needed in mountain resorts for the winter, and fishing guides are needed for the summer. Christmas tree lots love to have commissioned salespeople who can park their rigs in the middle of the trees and watch over them at night. Other salespeople follow trade shows or shopping mall promotions, manning booths and selling items to the public. Many traveling jobs would be impractical if you had to stay in hotels and eat in expensive restaurants.

Workamper News

At the same time RV travelers are looking for paid or volunteer jobs, employers are seeking employees who can supply their own housing for temporary or full-time positions. *Workamper News* brings everyone together. This publication started a few years ago as an eight-page newsletter to inform RV travelers of both volunteer and salaried jobs available to them. The first issues carried about 35 job announcements. Today *Workamper News* has grown to 24 pages with an average of more than 100 listings representing thousands of openings.

Some jobs listed pay salaries or hourly pay and other benefits, while others are volunteer positions with little more than free hookups. Not all help-wanted ads are exclusively for RV owners; some employers offer apartments or cottages for staff housing. The publication has been used by a wide variety of public and private enterprises with great success. Since the publishers try to weed out phony get-rich-quick schemes, most help-wanted ads are legitimate. Each listing includes location, duties, benefits, how to apply and who to contact. According to the publisher, there are often more jobs than people to fill them.

Other services the newsletter provides are situations-wanted ads (first 50 words free) and a résumé referral system. Résumés from active job-seekers are maintained on file and are scanned for those which meet the employer's requirements, such as skills, geographic location, benefits and length of employment.

The following jobs were advertised in a recent issue: A Montana dude ranch needed cooks, kitchen help, waiters/waitresses and housekeeping workers. A caravan-tour company wanted wagonmasters. Numerous mobile home parks and RV resorts wanted managers and maintenance personnel. Yosemite National Park wanted roomskeepers, food service workers, sales clerks and other employees. Yellowstone National Park wanted help in sales, grocery, food service, auditing, cooks and other jobs. Many state parks advertised for campground hosts, some with salary. A deluxe, four-star Florida beach resort offered full hookups in exchange for some grounds maintenance. Each issue also lists commission jobs, such as working Christmas tree lots, demonstrating computer software and selling resort lots. The number of job possibilities was impressive.

Volunteer Work

If you don't absolutely have to work to keep bread and beer on the table, why do it? You've done that all your life, so why continue to torture yourself? If you truly feel guilty about not "doing something" or if you get bored hanging around the house, try volunteering. You'll feel good about yourself. A special bonus is that your services will be sincerely appreciated and valued more highly than if you were to work in a fast-food restaurant or some other high-competition, low-pay job, trying to please an employer you don't like in the first place.

One of the major retiree volunteer organization is the Retired and Senior Volunteer Program (RSVP), sponsored by the federal ACTION agency. RSVP volunteers provides a variety of community pursuits helping old and young alike. Services include health care, companionship, security, education, and financial and social services at day care centers, nursing homes, schools, libraries, crisis centers, courts, and other community locations. RSVP volunteers operate runaway shelters, organize widows' support groups, and offer occupational counseling to first-time offenders. RSVP volunteers are usually paid expenses incurred while volunteering, such as transportation and other out-of-pocket expenses. They also receive accident and liability insurance while on service. For further information on the RSVP program, call the National Senior Service Corps at (800) 424-8867.

The federal ACTION agency also sponsors the Senior Companions Program (SCP). SCP volunteers assist mentally, emotionally and physically impaired elderly individuals by providing companionship, help with errands, financial counseling, health care, and nutritional assistance. The goal of Senior Companions is to help the elderly live independently at home for as long as possible. Senior Companions must be age 60 or older and low-income. In return for 20 hours of service each week, SCP volunteers receive a small tax-free allowance, a meal on the days they work, transportation, insurance, and an annual physical examination. To find out more about SCP, contact your local senior citizen center or the national ACTION office at ACTION, 1100 Vermont Av. NW, 6th Floor, Washington, DC 20525; (202) 606-4855

Enjoy the outdoors? As a U.S. Fish and Wildlife Service volunteer, you can find satisfying work in a nearby wildlife refuge or fish hatchery. Often it's possible to commute to the job site and back each day. Volunteer positions are often available to match your skills, abilities and preferences.

If you don't have to return home every afternoon, you might consider volunteering with the National Forest Service. There you will help maintain and improve the nation's forests and grasslands by doing light construction work, maintenance tasks, or clerical work. Depending on the job, you may reside on-site in a barracks, a mobile home, or conventional government housing.

To find out about volunteer programs with the Fish and Wildlife Service, call or write: U.S. Fish and Wildlife Service, 4401 North Fairfax Dr., Arlington, VA 22203; (703) 358-2043. To offer your services as a Forest Service volunteer, call or write: USDA Forest Service, Human Resources Program, P.O. Box 96090, Washington, DC 20090; (703) 235-8834.

Chapter Four

Cashing in Your Tax Investments

In the last chapter we discussed ways to work and earn money during retirement (and how to keep the better part of what you earn!). Now, we'll talk about money you've invested by way of paying taxes all these years, money that finally will be returned to you in one of three ways: Social Security, Social Security Disability or (for the very short of funds) Supplementary Security Income (SSI).

Don't for a moment think of these monthly checks as "charity." Today, for every dollar you earn, you pay 7.65 cents to Social Security, matched by your employer. You've invested many tax dollars over your lifetime, money deducted from your paycheck every week, money which has gone to help others before you. Now it's your turn.

We'll also investigate another way to draw down money you've invested over the years: the equity in your home. The money is just sitting there, fattening up your net worth, but not doing anything for your lifestyle. If your situation is like most folks', monthly house payments reduced your loan amount while steady appreciation increased the value of the home. This locked-up money could help finance your retirement, if you could only get at it. This route must be approached with caution, as we shall see, as potholes make it a dangerous road for the unwary.

Social Security

Despite continual efforts by some conservative congressmen to weaken, and even eliminate, Social Security, the program survives. These attacks are extremely short-sighted, because if they succeed in scuttling Social Security, millions of elderly would plunge below the already-low poverty line. The country's economy would suffer irreparable damage and the welfare system would stagger to its knees.

Social Security is the key to retirement for the vast majority of workers in our country. Without it, retirement would be impossible for them. Two-thirds of today's retirees depend on Social Security benefits for more than half of their monthly income. For millions, that's all there is. Without Social Security, an incalculable number would be forced to continue working until they drop dead or until the boss replaces them with younger employees. So rejoice that we have Social Security, and keep a jaundiced eye on any politician who wants to trash it.

We continually hear prophets of gloom and doom say, "Social Security won't be there when we need it." To hear them talk, the Social Security Administration is running out of money and will soon stop sending out checks. Nothing could be further from the truth. The fact is, Social Security is one of the few sectors of government that runs at a surplus. It takes in somewhere in the neighborhood of $5 billion a year more than it pays out. At the rate money is coming in and benefits are going out, income will cover outgo until the year 2013.

At that late date, it does look like the money flow will reverse course, and unless nothing is done about it, a crisis will occur in the year 2029. That's 35 years away, well past my retirement time. But you can be quite sure that something will be done. Half a dozen plans for coping with the problem are churning through Congress right now.

Social Security Eligibility

Qualifying for Social Security benefits is straightforward. You need to have earned a minimum amount of money for a minimum number of quarters and paid Social Security taxes on these earnings. The minimum number of quarters needed depends on your age, and the minimum amount of wages depends on the year worked. Before 1977, you needed to earn at least $50 in one three-month period to count that as a quarter. Beginning with 1978, you needed to earn $250, and the amount has increased each year until, in 1994, $620 earnings in a three-month period were required. The more money you earn, the higher your checks will be. If you work for yourself, and have been paying self-employment tax, that can qualify you for benefits.

Generally, anyone who has worked for ten years or more will qualify. If you were born before 1929, you will need less, as the following chart illustrates.

Birth Date	Minimum Years	Minimum Quarters
1921	8 years	32
1922	8 years, 3 months	33
1923	8 years, 6 months	34
1924	8 years, 9 months	35
1925	9 years	36
1926	9 years, 3 months	37
1927	9 years, 6 months	38
1928	9 years, 9 months	39

Figuring out how much your check will be is not so straightforward. Fortunately, the Social Security administration will assist you. The local office can help you make a request for a "Personal Earnings and Benefit Estimate Statement." Or you can call the Social Security Administration at (800) 772-1213 and request the form. When you receive your statement, make sure that all of your employers and all of your earnings are included. It isn't impossible that mistakes have been made. It's wise to check this periodically even if you are a long way from retirement, just to make sure you're being credited properly. After all, benefits are based on the highest of the last 35 years' earnings, so missing a year's worth of earnings might cause a reduction in benefits of $10 to $15 per month.

The form will ask you to make an estimate of your average earnings between now and retirement. Just put down your present earnings. That way you'll receive an estimate in today's dollars, which gives you a better idea of what your retirement picture will look like. When you receive your Personal Earnings and Benefit Estimate Statement it will also show you how much you would earn, in today's dollars, if you retire early.

Retirement at What Age?

Normal retirement is at age 65, at which time you'll receive a "full benefit" for your time worked. The earliest time you can retire is at age 62, but your monthly benefits will be reduced by 20 percent. For example, if you would receive $960 a month at age 65, at age 62 you'd be entitled to $768 a month. But for each year you wait to retire after age 65, you'll get an additional 4.5 percent added to your benefits. So if you wait until age 70 to retire, your check would be $1,176 per month.

Those who were born after 1938 will find their checks shorted for early retirement and won't get full retirement credits until they reach the age of 67, instead of 65. That's one of the ways Congress is dealing with the crisis that will be upon us in 2029.

So when do you retire? The difference between the $960 you might receive at age 65 and the $768 at age 62 means almost $200 a month less pension—for the rest of your life. But on the other hand, you'll receive $27,684 during those three years of early retirement. You'll be ahead of your co-worker who waits until 65 to retire, and you'll stay ahead until he or she catches up with you at age 77.

For many, the decision about when to collect Social Security is difficult. Obviously, if you plan on working after retirement and earning lots of money, you're going to have to give money back to the government. Remember, if you are under 65, you're only allowed to earn $8,040 before you start paying back one dollar for every two earned. However if you can work part time, and not go over the limit, you should come out ahead. Another point is: waiting until 65 to retire adds three more higher-income years to your record and gives you a slightly higher benefit check. But, you'll miss out on three years of retirement. Decisions, decisions!

Workers who hang on to their jobs until age 70 not only earn more credits, but can draw their Social Security benefits and continue working. Also, don't forget that the amount of your benefits increases with each year worked after age 65. For example: if you are 65 in 1995, for each year you work up until the age of 70, you'll gain a 4.5 percent increase in your benefit check. For five years your $960 benefit would grow to $1,176, an extra $122.50 a month. But then, had you retired at 65, you would have drawn $34,560 by the time you reached the age of 70. More decisions!

Social Security Disability

You don't have to be 62 or over to draw Social Security if you should become disabled or blind. The key to this is when a doctor or doctors certify that you are "totally and permanently disabled for a period of not less than one year." No matter what your age, you will draw benefits at the same rate as a person who is 65 years old and who has earned the same amount of credits as you. These benefits are paid regardless of your financial situation or how much other income you have each month. After two years on disability, you are also entitled to apply for Medicare, as if you were 65 years old.

To encourage you to return to work once you have recovered sufficiently, the government permits you to work on a trial basis, for a limited amount of time, without penalty. That is, you receive your disability payments and your salary for this period.

However, be aware that obtaining disability status is not easy, particularly if your disability is the least bit marginal. Because so many people have faked disabilities in the past, the Social Security Administration takes a hard look at each case and will disallow all but the most obvious disabilities.

For a time, even those were routinely turned down and most applicants forced to appeal.

To qualify for disability you must prove that you have a severe physical or mental impairment (or combination of the two) and will be unable to do any "substantial gainful activity" for a year or more. Where difficulty most often arises is in interpreting the terms "substantial gainful activity." Social Security administrators define this as any work that would pay at least $500 a month. According to their philosophy, all that's necessary is that you are capable of performing work that would pay $500 a month, even though such work is not available, and even though an employer probably wouldn't hire you if there were work available.

When a close relative of mine applied for Social Security Disability and was turned down, a case worker explained it to me this way: "Let's suppose a stock broker who earns $50,000 a year receives a brain injury and is no longer able to work as a broker. If he were capable of working as a dishwasher, then he could not be considered disabled under our rules. The fact that dishwasher jobs aren't available doesn't enter into the matter. We can only consider the question: Is the applicant capable of working?"

Remember, the key to collecting disability is to have a doctor, or more than one doctor, willing to testify that you have "severe physical impairment that prevents you from doing substantial gainful activity for a year or more." Often, when someone applies to a Social Security office for disability, a case worker will offer to get the medical evidence for you, to save you the trouble and expense of going to a doctor yourself. From personal experience I can advise you: get your own evidence from your own doctor!

To avoid approving the claim, case workers have been known to take affidavits from doctors who are sympathetic to the government's side—who barely know anything about your case—and then ignore your personal physician who could testify that you are disabled. It's not surprising that so many genuinely disabled have to go through the appeal process.

If you feel that you are truly disabled, by all means, appeal the decision. An average of 60 percent of all disallowed applicants win on appeal. You don't need to have an attorney for an appeal, but should you decide that you want one, get a lawyer who works on contingency (if you get nothing, he gets nothing).

Are You Missing a Pension?

Many people have pensions coming and don't realize it. Happily, there is a government agency working to locate "missing people" who are eligible for defined-benefit pensions (pensions that assure a fixed benefit) but who are not receiving them.

Some are spouses of deceased workers who are entitled to some part of his or her pension but don't realize it. Others know they earned a pension but figure it's lost because their employer went bankrupt. Still others are victimized when companies, facing financial difficulties on the way to bankruptcy, let their record-keeping fall apart or deliberately misappropriate the pension funds.

Martin Slate is executive director of the Pension Benefit Guaranty Corp., a federal agency that insures the private pensions of 41 million workers and takes over when a private pension plan is terminated without sufficient money to pay the promised pensions. Slate says, "Our central mission is to make sure everybody who's owed a pension gets one." The agency recently stepped up its search efforts for missing pensioners. Currently, the agency is paying benefits to about 160,000 retirees, and they're finding an additional 1,000 "lost" retirees each year.

If you can't locate a former employer who promised a pension, or if you believe your employer may have switched or terminated your defined-benefit plan, you may contact the Pension Benefit Guaranty Corp. for help. The address: PBGC Admin. Review and Tech. Assistance Div., 1200 K St. N.W., Washington, DC 20005.

Another source of retirement income you may overlook are Social Security benefits based on your ex-spouse's earning records. This is particularly important in the case of divorced women, who typically qualify for much lower Social Security benefits than their higher-paid husbands.

It turns out that you are eligible for benefits based on your spouse's records, even if he is not retired, if you fulfill the following requirements:

1. You are age 62 or older.

2. You were married to your ex-spouse for at least 10 years, and the divorce is at least two years old.

3. You haven't remarried, or you remarried someone who is receiving Social Security benefits as a widower, widow, parent or disabled child.

Your monthly check will be the same as if your earning record were the same as your spouse's. Of course, if you earned more than your spouse, forget it.

Supplementary Security Income

If your monthly income is exceptionally low and you aren't eligible for Social Security or Social Security Disability—Supplementary Security Income (SSI for short) can come to your rescue. To qualify for SSI you must be 65 or older or disabled or blind, and you must have little or no income. It's important to note that SSI isn't just for the elderly, it can be paid at any age as long as the applicant meets the above standards. "Blind" doesn't necessarily mean totally blind; very poor vision will sometimes qualify you. "Disabled" doesn't mean confined to a wheelchair, either; if doctors agree that you have a physical or mental problem that keeps you from working and is expected to last at least a year or to result in death, you may qualify. The rules are similar to Social Security Disability.

The basic SSI check is $407 for a single person and $610 a month for a couple (in 1991). Some states add money to that amount. In addition, folks who qualify for SSI usually also qualify for Medicaid and food stamps.

The financial qualifications vary from state to state, but basically, your total income must be less than $427 for one person and $630 as a couple. Some items of income don't count against you, for example: the first $65 of your earnings every month, food stamps, food, clothing or shelter from private non-profit organizations and most home energy assistance. There are other exemptions, which your local welfare office can explain. You also cannot have assets that exceed $2,000 for singles or $3,000 for couples. Again, some assets are exempt, which will be explained when you apply.

Reverse Mortgages

The idea of a "reverse mortgage" started in California, where highly inflated property values shelter huge sums of untouchable equities. Many folks who bought their homes 40 years ago for $20,000 now are living in the same home, but it's paid for, and it's worth $300,000. Since the property was bought long before California's "Prop 13" property tax law went into effect, taxes on the house are almost nothing, often less than $500 a year.

When retirement rolls around, unless the retirement income is adequate, you could be "house-poor." Some decisions need to be made. Should you sell the house, pay taxes on the profit (less the $125,000 exclusion) and pull down the equity for retirement? But then where do you live? Should you move to a less expensive area locally, which may be a less desirable neighborhood, or do you move to a cheaper part of the country altogether? But what if you like your neighborhood and love your home? It doesn't make sense to sell and move away, does it?

One answer for those with huge equities is to take the value built up in their homes and turn it into a reliable monthly income through a "reverse mortgage." Instead of paying a monthly installment payment to the bank, the bank sends you a monthly check, adding that amount to the total debt, or mortgage, against your home. An FHA-insured reverse mortgage can provide a flexible range of loan advance options, which may be combined or changed at any time.

Be careful, though—a reverse mortgage isn't a simple solution. You'll need to be quick with your calculator and be aware of sharks out there feeding in this huge pool of home equities, an ocean of an estimated $700 billion.

A reverse mortgage promises you a stipulated monthly payment based on three factors. First: the amount of equity held in your home. Second: an annual percentage rate applied against that equity. And third: your life expectancy.

Basically there are three kinds of reverse mortgage loans:

1. A "tenure plan," which pays a fixed monthly cash advance for as long as you live in your home. You can stay until you die, and then the home is sold, the bank takes its money, and the remainder, if any, goes to the heirs. By the way, this mortgage bears a compound interest rate, with interest being charged on accumulated unpaid interest.

2. A "term plan," which pays a fixed monthly cash advance for a specific time period. The cash advances stop when the term ends, but you are not required to repay the loan until you die, sell your home, or move permanently away. Short-term mortgages are practical if you plan on living in your home for five or six years and then moving to a retirement community. You can then sell the house, pay off the loan and have something left over for your new lifestyle.

3. A "line of credit plan," which lets you decide when to draw advances and how much of your home equity to use. Interest accumulates only on the money you draw.

The difference between regular home-equity loans and reverse mortgages is that home-equity loans usually require proof of a certain amount of income and require installment payments over a specified length of time, usually ten or 15 years. With a reverse mortgage, lending institutions are secured by a first trust deed on the home so they don't care about your income. They're protected because a home owner typically reverse mortgages between 30 and 80 percent of the home's equity. When the borrower moves or dies, whichever comes first, the house is sold and the mortgage paid off with the proceeds of the sale. Payments aren't taxable, and they don't affect Social Security benefits. Interest on the reverse mortgage is debited from the equity.

As in any financial transaction of this complexity, you'll find lenders all too willing to take advantage of our ignorance. They come up with outrageous calculations based on unrealistic life expectancies and/or saddle the homeowner with high interest rates that quickly eat up the equity. In some cases, the borrower finds his home drained of value, with zero equity, by the time the agreed-upon term is up. This can be serious; you'll not have any equity in your home to pay for your spouse's nursing home care (or your care) and nothing to leave your grandkids.

Another trap is a clause that the lending institution is entitled to 50 percent of any appreciation in your property over the term of the loan. Don't go for this.

If a reverse mortgage sounds like the answer for your situation, take steps to protect yourself. First, request the free 47-page booklet "Homemade Money" by mailing a self-addressed postcard to AARP Home Equity Information Center, 601 E Street NW, Washington, DC 20049. This will give you an idea of how to shop for a reverse mortgage.

Also, be aware that there are government-backed reverse mortgages which originate under a Department of Housing and Urban Development program. HUD loans carry no appreciation clause. Closing costs on a HUD reverse mortgage are generally less, too, costing approximately $4,000, compared with $5,000 or more for conventional loans.

If you are 62 or older, the Federal Housing Authority is offering to insure reverse mortgages through September 1995. The insurance guarantees payments even if a lender goes bankrupt or if the home's market value falls below the loan balance. Insured amounts vary, from $67,500 in rural areas up to $151,725 for metropolitan addresses. On a $100,000 home, FHA insurance costs would come to about $2,000.

To find a reverse mortgage lender in your area, call the FHA at (800) 732-6643. The FHA can also refer you to a

HUD-approved independent counselor, who can check the terms of a reverse mortgage, analyze your financial situation and advise you whether you to go for this arrangement or not. The counselor can also give you a list of HUD-approved lenders.

Other Ways to Tap Equity

More conventional ways to spend some of your home equity are refinancing your home, taking out a second mortgage or taking out a home equity line of credit. All three of these strategies require that you make monthly installment payments on your loan. And, since the loan is secured by your home, you could face foreclosure if you can't make the payments for any reason. If you're on a shoestring budget, you may be hesitant to do this. You are also responsible for loan fees and points the lender charges.

A more creative way of drawing your equity and staying put in your home is through a "sale leaseback." The idea is this: you sell your home to an individual for a substantial down payment and monthly installment payments over the term of the mortgage. In return, you receive a lease for the term of the mortgage. Your lease payments will much less than the house payments you will be receiving because the purchaser will be paying interest on the loan.

Normally this type of sale leaseback transaction is done between parent and adult offspring. Let's suppose you sell it to your daughter. She knows she will be getting the property anyway, but in the meantime, she can be taking deductions on interest, taxes, property maintenance and depreciation. These breaks, along with the rent you pay makes it painless for her to help you, because it won't cost her any money. (In order to do this, the sale price of the home should be at a fair market value, and your rent should be a fair market rent.) Should you die before the mortgage runs out, she will inherit the property, and the mortgage is moot. By that time there's probably been appreciation, so your daughter will make money on the deal.

Another way to do this is to have the buyer take out a conventional loan through a bank to purchase the property. In this case, you would receive all the proceeds from the sale and can use this money to invest in a safe, income-producing investment to help out with retirement expenses.

You'll need a family lawyer to make out the papers and ensure that both parties are protected. You'll want to be sure you have a lifetime lease with full rights to share the house with whomever you please. The contract must have a clause requiring subsequent buyers to honor that lifetime lease. You'll also want a rent control clause which limits rent increases to the cost of living index, and another clause that makes the buyer responsible for taxes, insurance and repairs.

Chapter Five

Now It's Your Turn!

All your life you've paid federal income tax and, most likely, state income taxes as well. Maybe you've even been nicked for city or county income taxes. If you own property, you don't have to be told that you've paid a wagonload of dollars to city, county and state governments over the years. If you didn't own property, and just rented a house or apartment all your life, don't feel smug and think that you've avoided paying property taxes. Actually, you've graciously included taxes in your monthly rent payments. The landlord simply paid the money over to the government for you and took a tax deduction for his trouble. When his taxes went up, so did your rent.

Now, add to this amount the state, county and city sales taxes you've paid over your lifetime, as well as miscellaneous hidden taxes and fees, and you begin to get an idea of how much money you've paid to keep your government in clover. You'll never know for sure, because every time you buy something from the store, the cost of the manufacturer's taxes are passed along to you as part of the purchase price: corporation taxes, sales taxes, property taxes, import duties, payroll taxes and who knows what else.

You've often wondered what the hell they do with all this money, haven't you? (If you haven't, you must have an exceptionally high threshold of pain.) We often hear politicians taking cheap shots at food stamps, Medicare, Social Security and other programs as being wasteful. If you listen carefully to their solutions, you'll find that we could solve all our budget problems simply by cutting back on programs that help the elderly, the needy and the unfortunate, while decreasing taxes for the well-to-do. Congress doesn't hesitate to spend our money to bail out wealthy corporations or on ever-increasing benefits for themselves. They take our surplus Social Security money and spend it on current budget items to reduce the deficit and then advocate cutting back on benefits and cost-of-living increases for retirees because "we can't afford it."

Payback Time

Even though an enormous amount of taxes are wasted, we have to recognize that a great deal of money is spent correctly. Without police and fire protection, highways, libraries, schools and health services, our lives would be very different. Without Medicare, Social Security and other programs for senior citizens, prospects for retirement would be indeed grim. We can probably agree, not all tax money is spent on boondoggles. This brings us to the focus of this chapter: what government and private services are out there for senior citizens and how to get your share.

"Wait a minute," I hear you saying, "some of those services sound like charity. Charity is for losers, not for me!" Well, perhaps some of this sounds like charity, but the cold fact is that you have paid for these services all your life. You've paid through taxes, club dues, United Way contributions and money in the Sunday collection plate. All these years, you've subsidized tasty meals at the local senior citizens' center, paid for card tables and bridge prizes and home care and meals-on-wheels for invalids. If you don't participate, it's like putting money in a bank and failing to take it out when you most need it. Now that's being a loser! It is of utmost importance that those forced to retire on limited budgets participate in these worthwhile senior citizen services. It makes retirement on a shoestring much easier.

The food stamp program is one of the tax-funded services designed to help low-income citizens. Yet, for some reason, many folks look down their noses at food stamps. They feel as if food stamps are a form of panhandling or charity. One reason for this negative impression is the continual harping by political opportunists who see this as a way to increase their popularity with voters. These political charlatans drop hints that food stamp recipients are guilty of crimes or immoral conduct when they receive stamps and then use them to buy food for the table.

The fact is, food stamp money comes from the Department of Agriculture and has nothing whatsoever to do with welfare (which is financed largely by property taxes). These same Department of Agriculture funds go to wealthy farmers who receive huge checks for raising certain crops and for not growing others. Huge corporate farms collect millions of dollars of Department of Agriculture money, in the form of crop insurance and assistance of all kinds. Dairy farmers received millions to slaughter milk cows so the government could cut down on the amount of surplus cheese. These same funds are used lavishly to pay subsidies to gentlemen farmers who grow tobacco for cigarettes and chewing tobacco. Ironically, a number of subsidized tobacco fields belong to medical doctors; it's a great tax dodge.

We rarely hear criticism of Agriculture Department subsidies for the wealthy. But we hear plenty about "welfare queens" who drive Cadillacs and buy groceries with food stamps. Well, it turns out that if a person owns an automobile that's worth more than $4,500, it is counted against the food stamp applicant as cash assets, which affects eligibility. So, don't be upset when some out-of-work housewife happens to drive a beat-up old Caddy to the supermarket.

Food stamp eligibility requirements change with the Consumer Price Index. At the end of 1994, the rules went something like this: for folks over 60, a single person can have no more than $756 a month in gross income, and a couple no more than $1,022 per month. This includes Social Security payments. A single person can have no more than $2,000 in cash or assets that can be turned into cash (stocks, IRAs, etc.). For couples, the maximum is $3,000. Can we agree that if a couple earns less than $1,022 a month, including their Social Security benefits, they deserve all the help they can get?

A home is not counted as a cash asset, but an automobile is, if it is worth over $4,500. There is a complicated formula for figuring just how much of the excess is counted as assets. An interesting note: a motorhome or a travel trailer is considered an asset when valued over $4,500, unless you live in it! Then it's considered your residence and doesn't count against food stamp eligibility. But you have to live in your rig more than half of the year.

With the strict eligibility for qualifying for food stamps, the surprising thing is just how many folks in the United States are qualifying. During the recession of 1991-1992, government officials stated that one out of ten citizens qualified for food stamps. So, if you are not receiving food stamps, please do not look down on those who do. If you must be angry with someone, take it out on the wealthy farmers and the Department of Agriculture. Should you qualify, by all means, demand your rights. You've always paid your share, and now it's your turn.

Senior Citizen Services

Some communities have highly successful programs that can make a world of difference in people's lives. For many retired folks, a well-run senior center is their focal point, a place to enjoy free medical services and nutritious meals, as well as social activities and a host of other free benefits. Senior citizen centers help make shoestring retirement possible.

The surprising thing about these community services is that so few retirees take full advantage of them. Recently, when doing research at a particularly attractive senior center, we asked the director what she considered to be her biggest problem. She replied, "Getting the news out that we exist! Folks just have no idea of what we offer. We send out mailings, and we ask our people to spread the word among their low-income neighbors. Many of our services are free, some have a nominal cost, others have a sliding fee, according to the ability to pay. Some items are limited to lower-income folks, but most are available to all. Yet we can't seem to spread the news!"

She then began listing the things senior citizens are entitled to in her area, most of them just for the asking:

Adult day care. Volunteers visit homes of caregivers to provide respite care and assistance as needed. This is a lifesaver for a spouse who is tied down with taking care of his or her partner. It provides a chance to go shopping or enjoy a movie or some outside recreation without having to worry about the partner.

Adult family homes. Room and board are offered in a licensed residential environment for the senior requiring some assistance with daily living tasks. This is also an option for the single person who hasn't the resources or the resignation to go to a "nursing home."

Adult protective services. Abuse, neglect, exploitation or abandonment are investigated, and short-term emergency support is given to adults in need of protection.

Advocacy program. Volunteers give help with forms, applications and appeals, plus advice on how to handle bureaucracy. Free civil legal services by volunteer attorneys are available to eligible, low-income clients. No child custody, criminal or litigation cases are accepted.

Alzheimers support group. Provides counseling, information and support for families. This is very important for those frustrated by an inability to get help.

Blind or impaired vision services. Offers a variety of services to the blind of all ages. "Talking" books are featured as a part of this program.

Blood pressure checks. Free monitoring of blood pressure is provided by volunteers.

Chore and in-home care service. Assistance with household tasks, shopping, meal preparation, personal care and transportation to medical appointments. Sliding fees make it affordable and help keep folks out of expensive health-care institutions.

Clothing bank. Provides suitable clothing for senior citizens. Donations come from closets of well-off members of the community, so the quality of the clothing is very good.

Dental care. This program provides low-income seniors with reduced-cost dental care.

Educational opportunities. A variety of classes—everything from aerobics to art, health and nutrition, water exercise and driver's education—are available to seniors free or for a minimal fee.

Employment. These are special programs for seniors, with on-the-job training, part-time employment and job-search assistance.

Financial assistance. Information and support concerning Medicaid assistance, Social Security problems and general financial assistance for low-income aged, disabled and/or blind individuals are available.

Food bank. Food is given to elderly in need or in emergency situations. Some of the food comes from government surplus commodities, some from donations by local businesses, the rest from community funds.

Food stamps. Low-income seniors eligible for these food coupons are offered help with the process.

Health care. Immunizations, diabetes-, hearing- and blood pressure-screenings, as well as a tuberculosis clinic and a low-cost program of foot-care clinics are located throughout the county. Financial assistance is available for those in need of a hearing aid.

Home-delivered meals. This is the famous Meals-on-Wheels for home-bound seniors over 60. A donation of $1.50 per meal is suggested, but only if the person can afford it.

Home health care. Skilled nurses visit the home, as well as physical therapists. This is covered either by Medicare, Medicaid, private insurance, or on a sliding fee scale for low-income people.

Hospice program. Hospice works to enable the patient to stay in his or her own home, providing education and emotional support for the terminally ill and their families.

Legal services. Free legal services are provided to older persons regarding their civil rights, benefits and entitlements. There are reduced fees for simple wills and community property agreements.

Low-rent housing. In this particular town there are over 300 units, ranging from efficiencies to small houses, that are managed by the county Housing Authority. They are limited to low-income adults aged 62 or more or senior couples (at least one aged 62 or more). There is currently a waiting list for vacancies, but mortgage assistance is also available.

Medical equipment. Loans are made to eligible individuals.

Nutrition. Lunches for seniors are served at noon Monday through Friday. The suggested donation of $1.50 is not expected of those who cannot afford it. Also, as previously mentioned, hot meals are sent to home-bound seniors through the Meals-on-Wheels program.

Recreation. There are arts and crafts, card games, poker, dances and any number of recreational programs.

Transportation. Door-to-door transportation for eligible seniors takes them shopping, to libraries and on errands. Volunteers provide transportation to doctors' offices, therapy sessions and to hospitals.

There's More!

Other services we've found in some communities are:

Adopt-A-Senior program. Volunteers provide socialization and transportation assistance for those who are socially or geographically isolated and need assistance to meet daily living needs.

Companion program. Volunteers provide social contact and support for elderly persons who show signs of confusion or weakness. Services include shopping, visiting, running errands and providing brief respites for caregivers.

Emergency rent assistance. Helps low-income elderly when an eviction notice has been served and when all other state and local resources have been exhausted.

Energy assistance. This program informs seniors about utility discounts and rebates to which they are entitled and administers a federally funded program designed to assist low income households during the winter months. It helps pay heating bills and assists homebound in completing applications.

Guardianship. This program provides advocacy services for those who are no longer able to make decisions or access essential services for themselves.

Senior travel club. Day trips, overnight getaways and longer excursions are provided at very low cost.

Telephone reassurance program. Volunteer callers talk with home-bound seniors at pre-arranged daily times. This helps many invalids live independently and gives them confidence that someone in the community cares about their well-being. There are no fees for this service.

Transportation services. Some communities have wheelchair lift vans available by appointment for door-to-door transportation. Buses and vans running fixed routes to hospitals, clinics, dialysis services and other medical facilities are also common. Another aid is a door-to-door escort service for trips to doctors, shopping and other necessary excursions.

Where are these senior citizen services located? Depending upon the community, you can locate senior services at senior citizens' centers, community or civic centers, the local park district, colleges and universities, the YMCA or YMHA, YWCA or YWHA, and churches and synagogues. If you have difficulty locating services, call the Elder Care Locator at (800) 677-1116 for assistance.

The Elder Care Locator can also direct you to an office of the Senior Community Service Employment Program (if there's one in your area). This program helps low-income persons over age 55 find part-time work in community service. Often there's a job training program involved, for those who want to find employment in the private sector.

All Centers Are Not Equal

The senior citizen program described above is a splendid example of a community in action, providing quality services for its retired and elderly citizens. But be aware that not all organizations operate in the same manner. Before making a decision on where to retire, a visit to the local senior citizens' center is highly advisable. Talk to the director and staff and see what is provided and the spirit in which it is offered.

During our research, we were continually surprised at the wide differences between senior centers in the towns we visited around the country. In some places the levels of interest and quality of services were excellent—in others, next to nothing was available. The lesson is: all senior citizen centers are not equal.

For example, one center we visited served free coffee and doughnuts in the morning while arts and crafts programs were getting underway, as well as soft drinks in the evening at dances and card parties. Daily meals were delicious and tastefully served, with cooking done on premises by a staff of paid senior citizen workers. At least ten rooms were devoted to activities, including a library, conference and exercise rooms. Hundreds of enthusiastic senior citizens worked on volunteer or self-help programs, while city, county and federal government funds paved the way for success.

Another center, in a similar-sized town, consisted of nothing more than a small, single room with a couple of shabby card tables. The door was open for just a few hours every afternoon, mostly for poker games. As for meals, we were told that two churches served lunch—one day a week each—as did the local Elks Club and Lions Club, making a total of four meals during the week. Nothing was provided by the center itself; you had to go to the club or church center to be served. But, in addition to being away from the intimacy of the senior center, an automobile was required to get to the meals, which had the unmistakable aroma of charity. Instead of enthusiastic, caring staff members, we found more than one senior center manager who resented our taking up her time with an interview.

It's There for You

For senior citizens on limited budgets, these services can make the difference between making out nicely or having to scrimp by. The inexpensive (sometimes free) meals served at the senior centers are often not only nutritious and tasty, but are also served in a pleasant setting where you can visit with friends and make new ones.

If, God forbid, you have health problems, in-home care employees will perform household tasks necessary to keep you in a clean, safe environment. They will prepare meals, vacuum, change linens, do laundry, mop floors and clean sinks. In addition, they provide transportation and/or escorting to all types of medical services when public transit isn't available, even doing shopping and running errands when necessary. In-home care programs mean being able to remain at home during convalescence instead of being forced into expensive care facilities not covered by Medicare. These programs are funded by federal, state and local tax monies. Most of these programs aren't limited to low-income senior citizens, by the way. All ranges of income are eligible, although higher-income persons are sometimes required to contribute toward the service cost based on a sliding fee scale.

An additional benefit, of interest to those senior citizens who are in need of part-time work, is that the paid in-home care employees are often senior citizens themselves.

Volunteering

The most successful and energetic senior citizen centers all seem to have one thing in common: a large number of volunteers. Folks at these centers with high levels of services don't just sit back and wait for things to happen or for the government to do something for them; they get out and make things happen! Their enthusiasm is catching. It spreads to local officials, to local citizens and businesses, bringing everybody into the act. They get involved in local politics and let their voices and needs be known. (Politicians listen when voters speak.)

Therefore, the best way to help yourself in a senior citizen center is to volunteer and help others. I've discussed this in an earlier chapter, but it cannot be stressed too strongly. By volunteering, you gain a deeper sense of self-respect and well-being, and you build up a debt of gratitude which may well be repaid someday—when you need it most. Somewhere down the line, you will need help, and you will feel free to call in your debts.

Often, volunteer jobs have a way of working into paid positions. Always, you will widen your network of friends. And finally, you'll know that you aren't receiving charity, because you are giving just as much as you are receiving.

Sharing the Experience of a Lifetime

This is the motto of RSVP (Retired Senior Volunteer Program), one of the most exciting volunteer programs of all. Funded by the United Way Agency and other community and governmental funds, this volunteer program channels the talents and experiences of its members into invaluable service. Because of its flexibility, RSVP finds ways to utilize each volunteer's individual needs, interests and physical capabilities to the best interests of the community. There is no charge for their services.

Whenever you find a strong, active RSVP, you can be pretty sure of also finding dynamic and valuable services for senior citizens. On any given day, RSVP volunteers are found in schools, libraries, nursing homes, hospitals and many non-profit organizations. RSVP volunteers are especially helpful in providing respite service for families with problems such as stroke, Alzheimer's, Parkinson's, cancer, cardiac or respiratory diseases.

Senior Citizen Newspapers

Every community seems to have at least one senior citizen newspaper. These are valuable sources of information about what is going on in the community and what services are available for the asking. Not all of the help comes from federal, state and local government; many services are donated by charitable organizations, corporations and private enterprises.

At random I pick up an issue of a senior citizen newspaper from the tall stack of publications that we've collected in our travels. This happens to be a very non-commercial-looking publication; much of it appears to be typewritten (no doubt produced by volunteer labor), yet it is chock full of interesting information. In addition to chatty local news, this paper furnished its readers with the following information:

1. The fact that low-income housing applications are being accepted, plus the addresses and telephone numbers of the appropriate managing agencies.

2. News of a free legal seminar, in which an attorney will cover the subject of wills, the "right to die" and other matters of interest to retirees.

3. A list of senior citizen centers serving noon meals and the menus for the week at each center. (They look tasty!)

4. A notice that the local college is sponsoring an Elderhostel Program with some highly interesting classes. The important part of the announcement is that folks over 60, with a yearly income of less than $12,000, can attend the classes for only $50 a week, including tuition, room and meals!

5. A warning from the state insurance commissioner that many senior citizens are paying too much for Medicare premiums and deductibles—often $1,000 a year too much. He gives information on how to cut these overpayments.

6. Comprehensive guidelines for choosing a good nursing home. Ways to determine whether you will be happy there and whether the staff and management truly care about the patients over profits.

7. A list of volunteer opportunities through RSVP, including such diverse jobs as helping with a Kid Town fair, being a guide at a museum and blacksmith shop, as well as working at a disabled children's center.

8. A complete directory of community services, including transportation, legal aid, home-delivered meals, and health-related assistance such as a stroke patients' support group and programs for those suffering from Alzheimers or lung problems.

9. A list of community activities with a calendar listing potlucks, quilting classes, blood pressure clinics, exercise classes, pinochle games, dancing, senior singles clubs, senior softball games and much more. There were even free podiatry checkups for those who wear their feet out trying to attend all of these activities.

10. The monthly listing of the Senior Travel Club, which makes inexpensive trips to nearby tourist attractions, sometimes overnight, sometimes day trips.

Of further interest were the free classified advertisements. Readers offered to do house cleaning or to sell fishing rods and three-wheel motorscooters. One individual offered to sell a "complete cremation package, including transfer and storage of remains—$2,000 value discounted 50% for cash or trade for firearms of equal value."

Even though you probably aren't particularly interested in buying a second-hand cremation package, these local senior newspapers can put you in touch with what's happening in the community. You'll know whether you're getting your share of the benefits you used to provide for for others. Now it's your turn! (Now why would anybody want to trade a perfectly good cremation package for weapons???)

Medical Care U.S.A.

Thank heavens for Medicare! For years, rich insurance companies and wealthy medical practitioners—led by the American Medical Association—fought tooth and nail against Medicare and general health care reform. But in 1965, a surprisingly courageous Congress succeeded in making medical care for the elderly a right rather than a privilege. Medicare at last! Since that time, it's saved millions of elderly couples from disastrous poverty.

Today, however, an exceedingly cowardly Congress— bullied by the same bloated insurance companies, wealthy doctors and American Medical Association lobby—are afraid to do anything about health care reform. Some are actually in favor of dumping Medicare! Pardon my soapbox, but I get furious when I realize that the same million-aire senators who piously preach against reasonable health care, happily accept tax-paid coverage for their families, while allowing millions of families across the nation to do without. It also galls me to know that the United States is alone in the community of civilized nations without uni-versal health care. Even most third-world nations see to it that their citizens do not die from lack of medical care. Let's all give thanks to the 1965 Congress, and again, thank heaven above for Medicare!

Medicare Eligibility

How can you become covered by Medicare? Three con-ditions make you automatically eligible. First: when you reach the age of 65 and are receiving Social Security retire-ment benefits or Railroad Retirement benefits, you are automatically entitled to Medicare. Second: when you become 65 and your spouse is receiving Social Security—or you become 65 and your deceased spouse worked enough quarters to qualify—you are also automatically eligible. And third: at any age after you have been eligible for Social Security Disability payments for 24 months you automati-cally qualify. Note that the 24-month waiting period begins the date you were disabled, not when you first started receiving disability checks.

If you fall into one of these three "automatic eligibility" groups, you will be enrolled in the "Part A" Medicare pro-gram without filing an application or paying a premium. Part A benefits cover hospitalization, skilled nursing facili-ty services, home health care services and hospice care.

Three other groups are entitled to voluntarily enroll in the Part A Medicare program by filing an application. First: if you are 65 years or older and would be eligible for Social Security but are not drawing benefits; that is, you're still working or are not ready to retire for any reason—you can voluntarily enroll in Medicare and not pay any premium. Second: at any age when you, your spouse or any of your dependents has permanent kidney failure, that individual is also eligible for Part A Medicare without premiums, starting from the third month of dialysis, or from the first month if you participate in a self-dialysis program. And the third category: anyone over 65, who doesn't qualify for Social Security, can enroll and pay a $245-a-month premium (in 1994) for the A Plan coverage. However, this is fairly expensive; you might be better off with a private plan.

Note that if you don't fall into one of the "automatically qualified" categories, you must take it upon yourself to enroll. Even though you automatically qualify, don't wait for the government to act. To make sure you are protected when you retire, apply for Medicare three months before your 65th birthday. That way you'll be covered the month you turn 65. If you don't enroll within three months after your birthday, you can enroll later, during the first three months of each year but any premiums you pay will be 10-percent higher for each 12-month period that elapses since the time you first could have enrolled.

Two Parts to Medicare

Medicare comes in two segments: Part A and Part B. One part covers you while in the hospital, the second part takes care of you outside of the hospital. When you qualify for Medicare, you are automatically covered for hospitalization. But the out-patient portion of Medicare—the part that pays doctor bills, medicines and items of that nature—is optional. To make sure you receive all benefits possible, sign up for Part B as well. They'll deduct a small premium from your Social Security check, but it's worth it.

Everyone who qualifies for Medicare gets Part A benefits, which cover hospitalization, skilled nursing facility services, home health care services and hospice care. After a $100 deductible, Part B takes care of 80 percent of doctor bills, outpatient hospital services (such as emergency room visits), diagnostic tests, ambulatory surgery, laboratory services and pap smears. It also pays 80 percent of approved charges for occupational and speech therapy services and durable medical equipment and supplies. Items not covered are things like eyeglasses, hearing aids, dentures, or routine physical exams. It's important to know that you must apply for Part B. It isn't automatic *or* unlimited.

Medicare pays all approved charges for the first 60 days of inpatient hospital care in a benefit period (after you pay the deductible). Should the doctor not agree to accept Medicare's schedule of payments, you pick up the extra fees. As of the time of writing this book, the following payments are in effect:

For the 61st through the 90th day, Medicare pays all approved charges except for $174 per day which you pay. If you need more than 90 days of hospitalization in any benefit period, you have 60 "lifetime reserve days" which are not renewable; once you use them, they're gone. Each reserve day costs you $348. It also helps with 100 days of inpatient, post-hospital nursing facility care; Medicare pays for the first 20 days, then you pay $87 a day for the next 80 days. It pays all approved charges for medically necessary home health care. The catch here is what Medicare considers approved and what is not. Doctors often have different notions as to their worth than do Medicare officials. The bright side of this picture is Medicare covers most of the costs if a doctor certifies you as terminally ill and you are sent to a hospice until you kick the bucket. That oughta cheer you up.

Uncovered Expenses

Medicare Plan A doesn't cover telephones or televisions, private rooms or private duty nurses, and it won't pay for staying in a nursing facility if it is mainly personal care, such as help in walking, getting in and out of bed, eating, dressing, bathing and taking medicine.

Something you need to pay attention to is whether or not a hospital "participates" in Medicare. Participating hospitals are under contract with the government to accept Medicare reimbursement. Most hospitals do participate in Medicare, but you should confirm this with hospital admissions or the administrative office.

There is one condition when Medicare will cover you in a non-participating hospital: when you receive emergency care. This coverage is good only if going elsewhere would risk death or serious bodily harm, and only until the emergency passes. When the emergency is over, you must transfer to a participating hospital or you'll pay your own bills.

Medicare insurance isn't good in foreign hospitals, except that hospital services may be provided in Mexico or Canada, but only if you live closer to one of these hospitals than to a participating American hospital. This assumes that comparable services are not accessible in your United States neighborhood.

Medicare is a complicated subject. Knowing how the system works could be very important to your pocketbook. Your local Social Security office has several publications and pamphlets which describe in detail what you are entitled to. Regulations change from time to time, so you need to rely on your Medicare office and your local senior services agencies for up-to-date details.

You might want to order a copy of "The Medicare Handbook," publication #HCFA 10050, from the U.S. Department of Health and Human Services, 6325 Security Blvd., Baltimore, MD 21207. Also, AARP can supply you with information on the nearest Medicare/Medicaid Assistance Program. Write or call AARP at 601 E St. NW, Washington, DC 20049; (202) 434-2277.

An excellent publication—which should be available in your local library—covers the intricacies of Medicare in depth. This is Retirement Rights, the Benefits of Growing Older, by Nancy Levitin (Avon Books, New York, 1994).

Medigap Insurance

As you can see, Medicare has big gaps, holes which can suck up savings accounts in a hurry. Most people (who can afford it) purchase additional coverage, known as "Medigap," which is supposed to cover some or all of your extra medical costs. These come in the form of Medicare supplements and major medical policies sold by private insurance companies.

However, beware when purchasing this coverage. It's been a fertile field for con artists working for unscrupulous insurance companies. They high-pressure clients into buying more insurance than needed or policies that don't pay off as advertised. Be sure to order the free booklet, Guide to Health Insurance for People with Medicare (details in the Appendix). And don't let a suede-shoes salesman scare you into a policy that isn't right for you.

Medicaid, the Second-Level Safety Net

The tragic fact is not everyone who retires—voluntarily or involuntarily—qualifies for Medicare. What happens to them? Or, suppose you qualify and your spouse doesn't? It only takes a few trips through the money-sucking medical system to knock your finances into the gutter, to wipe out that nest egg you've worked so hard for all your life.

Fortunately, there's a second-level "safety net," a public assistance program that provides medical benefits to people who cannot afford to pay for their own health care. It's called Medicaid. This is a joint federal-state medical assistance program that squeaked through Congress along with Medicare back in 1964. Medicaid (called "Medi-Cal" in California) pays benefits to people who are blind, age 65 or over, or disabled, provided they meet certain strict financial eligibility requirements.

If you are retiring on a shoestring, with a budget to match, perhaps you'll be eligible immediately for Medicaid. However, even if you're in the fortunate position of earning too much money, the huge holes in Medicare's safety net can quickly remedy that.

The largest hole is nursing home stays. Since Medicare was designed to cover "skilled" medical care, it won't pay for "unskilled" or "custodial" care. Furthermore, Medicare only covers skilled nursing home costs if the patient enters after hospitalization. Less than 30 percent of nursing home patients enter that way. But it's these unskilled and custodial services that disabled patients desperately need, things like dressing, bathing, cooking, etc. Uncovered expenses for at-home care can easily run $2,000 a month, and nursing care $3,000 a $5,000 a month. It doesn't take long for your life savings to disappear. This is where Medicaid comes in. It turns out Medicaid has become the number one provider of long-term care for older Americans.

Unlike Medicare—which is relatively uncomplicated, either you qualify or you don't—Medicaid requires recipients to show a definite financial need. The ground rules to qualify for Medicaid are different from state to state, but all fall within general federal guidelines. If and when you qualify, Medicaid pays for prescription drugs, unskilled long-term care, and many other items normally not covered by Medicare.

It isn't only the indigent and elderly infirm who need to be aware of the Medicaid program. Even those who think of themselves as financially comfortable should know about steps they can take to protect themselves and shelter their life savings in the event they or their spouse require long-term care.

Who Is Eligible for Medicaid?

This is a very complicated question. Since Medicaid is a state and federally administered program, each state interprets the rules differently. Unless you fall into the class of very poor, you may need expert help in figuring out whether you are eligible for Medicaid. And if you don't qualify, the experts may be able to show you how. They can also tell you how to appeal an unfavorable decision.

In general, three categories of individuals may qualify for Medicaid. The first category is those who are aged, blind, or disabled and who are also receiving federal Supplemental Security Income (SSI) payments. They automatically qualify for Medicaid assistance. Some states, however, place additional restrictions on SSI recipients. If you live in Connecticut, Hawaii, Illinois, Indiana, Minnesota, Missouri, Nebraska, New Hampshire, North

Carolina, North Dakota, Ohio, Oklahoma, Utah, or Virginia—check with your local social services office for limitations.

The second category is financially needy individuals who are on Medicare, but cannot pay the premiums, deductibles, and co-payments because of low income. All states are supposed to pay this, provided the recipient qualifies under the Medicaid limits. But you have to request payment.

The third category is the medically needy—aged, blind or disabled patients—even though they have income in excess of the Medicaid limits but not enough income to pay their medical bills. However, many states won't pay if an applicant receives as little as a dime above the Medicaid income limits. The states that do not provide Medicaid coverage to "medically needy" applicants are: Alabama, Alaska, Arizona, Arkansas, Colorado, Delaware, Florida, Idaho, Iowa, Kansas, Louisiana, Mississippi Nevada, New Jersey, New Mexico, Oklahoma, Oregon, South Dakota, Texas, and Wyoming. In the states not listed, recipients are allowed to "spend down" their excess income on medical bills and then Medicaid benefits kick in when their income falls below Medicaid income limits.

Qualifying Medicaid Income Limits

All of your income from all sources is counted against your eligibility for Medicaid except the following: half of all earned monthly income, plus $65, and $20 of all unearned monthly income (that is money from Social Security, pensions, interest, etc.), and infrequent or irregular income. In effect, a single person can earn about $905 a month or $1,190 for a couple, depending upon individual state regulations.

As mentioned, if you live in one of the states not listed above, you can "spend down" your income on medical expenses. For example, if you are single and go over your Medicaid income limit by $300 a month, you can qualify for Medicaid in any month that you spend more than $300 on medical bills.

So far, the income limit seems straightforward. But if you are married and your spouse needs Medicaid the rules become complicated. It turns out that if the disabled spouse lives at home, a fairly low earnings limit applies, but if your spouse is in a nursing home, then your limit can be more generous than if he or she stays at home. The limit in this case could range from $1,200 to $1,800 a month, depending on the state and several other factors. All of this seems insane, because in most states Medicaid coverage of home care services is virtually nonexistent. And, even in states where Medicaid covers home care, you're often better off paying for your care at home privately for as long as possible. This is because in order to be covered, you must go to a nursing home that accepts Medicaid, and you must accept whatever care is offered.

Actually, the whole matter of Medicaid income limits is so complicated that those who are on the verge of qualifying are urged to consult their local Medicare/Medicaid Assistance Program office. Contact AARP, 601 E St. NW, Washington, DC 20049; (202) 434-2277, for the nearest office.

Medicaid Resource Limits

Here is another touchy area that may require expert help: determining whether your assets are near or over the limits. The amount of cash and property you can possess varies with individual state regulations. Generally, you are permitted to hold cash and property not to exceed $2,000 to $3,000 for a single person and $3,000 to $4,500 for a married couple.

Items which do not count against your eligibility are: 1) your home, which must be your primary residence; 2) household goods and personal effects; 3) an automobile up to a value of $4,500; 4) life insurance with a face value of up to $1,500; 5) a cemetery lot and $1,500 for burial expenses;

and 6) income-producing property (such as land you use to grow food for personal use.)

These exempt resources are subject to some conditions that may or may not be to your benefit, depending on how you handle your affairs. For example, your home is exempt, even if you move out of it, as long as it remains occupied by your spouse, or if you plan to return home after your illness. Yet sometimes state Medicaid officials add a qualification, that you realistically will be able to return.

Several strategies exist for qualifying for both Medicaid and SSI—maneuvers for bringing assets and income down which are devious-sounding, yet perfectly legal. You'll probably need a Medicaid legal practitioner or attorney who specializes in Medicaid before you take any such steps. Your senior citizen center or local bar association can refer you to such a specialist. If you're entitled to it, go for it; your taxes paid for it.

Free Medicare?

More than two million Medicare beneficiaries are paying too much for their Part B premiums. As much as a thousand dollars a year too much! It seems there are some "secret benefits" intended for low income retirees; "secret" because the state governments are keeping it quiet and saving money by not fulfilling their obligations under law.

It turns out that in 1988 and again in 1990, Congress enacted a "Qualified Medicare Beneficiary program" (QMB), which requires states, through their Medicaid programs, to pay Part B premiums for those whose incomes are at or below the poverty level, described as "financially needy." These are individuals who are on Medicare, but cannot pay the premiums, deductibles, and co-payments because of low income. All states are supposed to pay, provided the recipient qualifies under Medicaid.

In some instances they pay co-payments and deductibles. That is, if a patient qualifies, he or she isn't billed for some or all of the excluded charges. However, if you don't apply for this assistance, the state won't pay. They have no way of knowing your economic situation unless you speak up.

There are other Medicare and Medicaid benefits which accrue to very low income patients. If you are in this category you should inquire at the Medicaid office of your local department of human welfare or social services. The local senior citizens' center can supply you with directions. Should you have problems getting information, check in the phone book in the government section and look for your state or local agency on aging office. For a pamphlet describing eligibility, an application and other detailed information, send a self-addressed stamped envelope to Families USA, 1334 G St. NW, Washington, DC 20005. (See the Appendix for other Medicare publications available free of charge from the government.)

Chapter Six

Try Before You Buy

While doing research in the Midwest, I stopped over in a small Ozark town, one that had been praised highly as a retirement paradise by a popular retirement guide. It was a pleasant-looking place, with a friendly, small-town atmosphere and several excellent fishing lakes nearby.

Most of the folks I interviewed seemed to love the town. Property was inexpensive, the climate relatively mild and fishing was great. An added bonus was low property taxes. Retirees who had moved there from elsewhere mostly were happy with their decision. Then I happened to meet a man who retired there and who hated it. He was in the process of moving away. I asked why.

"I was born and raised in Philadelphia," he explained, "and I've always been used to the city. I like to sleep late in the morning and stay up late at night. If I wanted a snack at midnight, there was always a restaurant open, or if I needed something from the grocery store, there was one nearby that was open 24 hours. But here, everything shuts down at eight o'clock in the evening. I tried to learn how to fish, but I've never been able to get the hang of it. I just don't fit in here."

When asked why he made the decision to move here in the first place, he replied, "Well, I read about this town in a retirement guide. According to the book, it was one of the top-rated retirement places in the country. I had just gone through a divorce and decided this would be a great place to start over. It sounded pretty good on paper, but the book didn't say anything about this being a dry county. I was always used to having a couple of drinks after work and mingling with people. And, I like to order Cabernet Sauvignon with my prime rib, not Pepsi-Cola. Here, in order to have a cocktail, I have to drive 35 miles to the next county, go to a package liquor store, bring it home and mix it myself. I hate to drink alone!"

It turns out that a few weeks previously he received an invitation to a party from one of the few friends he had been able to make. His first social event. The party was in the next town, about 15 miles away, and he felt comfortable having a few drinks since a "designated driver" volunteered to drive everyone home after the party. Unfortunately, on the way home, the designated driver was stopped at a police roadblock. Even though the designated driver hadn't had a drink, the whole lot of them were tossed into jail. He was charged with "transporting drunks," his passengers charged with being intoxicated in public.

"I just don't fit in here," the retiree repeated sadly.

The lesson is: try it before you buy it. This unhappy man could have saved himself a lot of time, money and effort had he done some investigation on his own and not blindly accepted someone else's statistical evaluation. A trip to this dream town and a few nights in a motel would have told him everything he needed to know.

What Retirement Guides Don't Tell You

Many magazine articles and guidebooks that recommend retirement locations are written for an audience of fairly affluent people. Retirement writers tend to assume their readers live in an idealistic world of country clubs, fancy restaurants and split-level ranch homes. They'll count the number of museums, operas and symphony orchestras in a location and use them as criteria for a good place to retire. Of course, these amenities add a touch of class to your retirement location, yet, how many times a month will you be attending an opera, a symphony performance, or visiting a museum? Some retirees might consider the number of municipal golf courses, bowling lanes or public libraries far more important.

Retirement writers sometimes judge the quality of medical care by counting the number of doctors in the area, the amount of money invested in hospitals and the number of CT scanners available to physicians. Special praise goes to communities with a medical school. Frankly, I'm more interested in whether doctors are accepting new patients, the cost of an office visit and how much I will pay for a hospital room. Medical school? I'd prefer to have my vasectomy done by a journeyman doctor rather than by a nervous student, thank you very much.

Favorable ratings are often awarded on the basis of conditions that don't affect retirees. For example: good schools, high employment and a booming business climate leads writers to boost a town's popularity rating, while horrible weather and high taxes are often ignored. Quality grammar schools and juvenile recreational programs matter less to retirees than quality senior citizen centers and safe neighborhoods. And the problem with full employment and thriving business conditions is they result in high prices and expensive housing.

The bottom line is, by giving the same weight to concerts, museums and medical schools as to climate, reasonable housing costs and personal safety, the retirement picture becomes unrealistic for all but the affluent. What good is an opera house if you get mugged as you leave because the city is crime-ridden? What good are hospitals if they are so expensive that you go bankrupt before you can get across the lobby?

Some retirement guides are excellent sources for data on towns and cities that would otherwise be difficult to find. They can tell you a world of information that can help you decide whether a place is a viable candidate for retirement. But in the final analysis, you have to go there and see for yourself. You have to see what the retirement guide cannot tell you: will you love it, or will you hate it?

What to Look For

Following is a list of requirements my wife and I personally consider essential for a successful retirement relocation. Your needs may be different; feel free to add to or subtract from the list, and then use the list to measure communities against your standards.

1. Safety—Can you walk through your neighborhood without fearful glances over your shoulder? Can you leave your home for a few weeks without dreading a break-in?

2. Climate—Will temperatures and weather patterns match your lifestyle? Will you be tempted to go outdoors and exercise year-round, or will harsh winters and suffocating summers confine you to an easy chair in front of the television set?

3. Housing—Is quality housing available at prices you're willing and able to pay? Is the area visually pleasing, free of pollution and traffic snarls? Will you feel proud to live in the neighborhood?

4. Nourishment for your interests—Does your retirement choice offer facilities for your favorite pastimes, cultural events and hobbies, be it hunting, fishing, adult education, art centers, or whatever?

5. Social compatibility—Will you find common interests with your neighbors? Will you fit in and make friends easily? Will there be folks from your own cultural, social and political dimensions?

6. Affordability—Are goods and services reasonable? Can you afford to hire help from time to time when you need to? Will your income be high enough to be significantly affected by state income taxes? Will taxes on your pension make a big difference?

7. Medical care—Are local physicians accepting new patients? Does the area have an adequate hospital? (You needn't live next door to the Mayo Clinic; you can always go there if your hospital can't handle your problem.) Do you have a medical problem that requires a specialist?

8. Distance from family and friends—Are you going to be too far away, or in a location where nobody wants to visit? Would you rather they wouldn't visit? (In that case, you'd do better even further away.)

9. Transportation—Does your new location enjoy inter-city bus transportation? Many small towns have none, which makes you totally dependent on an automobile or taxis. How far is the nearest airport with airline connections? Can friends and family visit without driving?

10. Senior services—Senior centers should be more than merely places for free meals and gossip; there should be dynamic programs for travel, volunteer work and education. What about continuing education programs at the local college?

Using Your Vacations to Investigate

Ideally, you'll start your retirement search long before the day your company shakes hands and says goodbye. Instead of going to the same old place for vacations, try to visit someplace different each time. Look at each location as a possible place to live.

Even if you are already retired, you need to do some traveling if you plan on moving somewhere else. Your travels needn't be expensive. Pick up some camping equipment at the next garage sale in your neighborhood—a tent, sleeping bags and a cooking stove. Just about anywhere you want to visit will have either state parks with campgrounds or commercial camps—places like KOA—where you can pitch a tent. Many RV parks have special spots for tent camping. Your local library will have a campground directory to help you locate a place in or near your target town.

Check out real estate prices. Look into apartment and house rentals. Are there the kinds of cultural events in town you will enjoy? A cultural event could be anything from light opera to hoisting a glass of beer at the corner tavern; the question is, will you be happy you moved there? Just looking closely, as if you truly intended to move there, will tell you a lot.

While you are there, be sure to drop in on the local senior citizens' center. Talk to the director and the members of the center to see just what services will be available should you decide to move there. A dynamic and full-service senior center could make a world of difference in your everyday life.

A very important consideration is public transportation. Over the past few years a large number of smaller towns in the United States have been stripped of intercity bus service. The Greyhound Corporation was permitted to buy out its major competition, Trailways, and shut down all but the most profitable runs. If you choose to live in one of these towns, you ought to be aware that you will be totally dependent upon an automobile.

If some time in the future you are without a car—because you've become unable or cannot afford to drive—you'll be trapped. Your grandkids can't visit you by bus, and if the nearest airport is 100 miles away, you'll not be able to meet the incoming flight. They'll have no way to get from the airport to your home. Yes, you could take a taxi, but places that don't have bus services may not have a fleet of taxis at your disposal. Besides, by the time you make a few 200-mile round trips by cab, you could have purchased your own taxi. These conditions are something you probably wouldn't notice on a regular vacation. You can pick up on them if you pay attention though.

In investigating a town, one of your first stops should be at the local chamber of commerce office. A world of information can be found there. The level of enthusiasm and retirement advice offered by the chamber staff clearly tells you something about the town's elected officials' and businessmen's attitudes toward retirees. Most chamber offices love to see retirees move into their towns; they recognize the advantages of retirement money coming into the economy and the valuable contributions retirees can make to the community. These offices will do just about anything to help you get settled and to convince you that living in their town is next to paradise. However, don't be surprised if the person behind the counter isn't the least bit interested in your idea of retiring in their town. My experience has been that a few chamber of commerce offices are staffed with minimum-wage employees who seem to resent folks coming in to ask questions and interfering with the novels they are reading. When this is the case, you can guess that the level of services and senior citizen participation in local affairs could be somewhat inadequate.

Newspaper Research

Between periods of travel, you can do your research at the local library or by mail. Almost all libraries have out-of-town newspapers. The larger the library, the wider the variety.

If you live in a small town where your library can't provide the newspapers you want (particularly those from another state or smaller towns some distance away), one way to obtain them is to write to the chamber of commerce in the place you are interested in and explain that you need a copy or two to make decisions about retiring there. You can also write to the newspaper office (look in the phone directory section of your library for the local phone book and the name of the paper). Some real estate brokers will gladly mail you copies of the local newspaper, because they know you will probably use their services when and if you decide to buy. We once had a real estate office send us a three-month subscription to the local paper to help us make up our mind.

A newspaper becomes a very valuable research tool. The most important section in an out-of-town paper is always the classifieds. Here you can check the prices of homes, rentals and mobile home parks. Compare them with your hometown newspaper and you begin to get a picture of relative costs.

Look at the help-wanted ads and compare them to the work-wanted ads. You can see what the offered wages are, as well as the wages people are asking. This gives you an indication of what kind of earnings you can expect, should you look for part-time work, as well as what kind of competition you will have for jobs. Some classified pages have a special heading for "managers wanted," where you'll find positions managing apartment buildings, motels or trailer parks. Typically, these jobs offer free rent and perhaps a salary in return for a minimum amount of management work. Be careful, however, that you don't end up working full time just for rent!

If mobile home parks advertise spaces for rent, you know that the situation should be okay for buying a mobile home. If there are no rental spaces available, you might find conditions where mobile homes will depreciate sharply. Compare the prices of used items such as furniture, appliances and automobiles against your paper's classifieds. If they are much higher, you can figure the cost of living is also higher.

Check the rest of the paper to get a flavor of what the town is like. See if supermarket prices compare to those at home, particularly if the same national chains operate in both places. Sometimes identical specials will priced differently; this also tells you something about the cost of living.

Look at the newspaper's editorial pages to observe the publisher's political stance. It's very interesting how this can influence the thinking of a community. Look over the news stories to see if they are heavily slanted politically instead of trying for a neutral position. Particularly revealing are campaigns for or against services and spending for senior citizen and low-income residents.

If you are uncomfortable with the direction of the political slant, this may be something you can investigate when you arrive in the town. It's impossible to tell for sure how local people think or vote by the way a newspaper presents its opinions, but often—when this paper is the only source of local news—these opinions are accepted as fact. If you have strong political views, you might feel uneasy in a community where you are in a tiny minority. See, too, how crime is reported; the way a paper reports crime news tells you something about a town's safety.

Newspapers should list senior citizen activities, cultural events like lectures and free concerts and often give news of community college classes open to seniors. Look for this menu of activities. See which ones are free, which ones cost money and which activities might interest you. A newspaper with a large section devoted to senior citizen news indicates a high level of interest in the well-being of retirees. Look for retiree political action groups. Wherever senior citizens band together to vote, the level of services and benefits rise in proportion to their numbers.

Out-of-town telephone books are valuable adjuncts to newspapers for information. You can check for retirement homes and apartment complexes that cater to seniors and get the address of the local housing authority office. If there is such a thing as subsidized housing available, they can tell you how to find it and how to apply.

A telephone book's Yellow Pages can give you a picture of the business life in town. The number of banks, supermarkets, shopping centers and other commercial entities tells you something about the vitality of business. This is where you check for bus service and taxi companies. Look under the listing for "airlines" or "airports" to see if there is a local airport and which airlines service it. A telephone book also gives an up-to-date listing for the chamber of commerce office and the senior citizens' center. A letter to each of them could yield valuable information about the locality. A non-reply also tells you something.

After you've researched a community thoroughly by library research, you still need to visit in person.

Chapter Seven

Weather, Crime and Your Budget

For many people, retirement means moving to a warm climate. After experiencing a lifetime of freezing winters, they dream of living someplace where they'll not have to shovel snow or change to special tires every November and back to regular tires in March. They know they'll love warm winters because they've sometimes managed to spend a week or two of their precious vacation time in Phoenix or St. Petersburg during the dead of winter. Expensive, but worth it for many folks.

They'd love to live in the Sunbelt full time, but put off moving until after retirement. Finding a job in a desirable, warm climate is sometimes difficult. Problems arise when too many others make the move to desirable climates—job competition becomes intense and working conditions and wages are usually substandard. So, working people tend to postpone moving to that idyllic climate until retirement.

But when that looked-forward-to day finally arrives, unless retirees have a more-than-adequate retirement income, many abandon that dream of Florida, Arizona or California retirement. They remember those high-priced vacation interludes. They read in newspapers and magazines that these places are super-expensive. "I can't afford that," they say, as they make plans on toughing it out every winter for the rest of their lives.

If they'd consider the facts carefully, they might discover that suffering cold weather isn't necessary after all. The interesting thing is, depending on how you do it, retirement in a benign climate can cost less than staying at home.

There's no reason you can't enjoy a shoestring retirement in Florida, California or any of the other warm-winter places.

This is true for several reasons. For one thing, heating costs are obviously much lower in warmer climates. Furthermore, low wages don't matter to a retiree who doesn't need to work. On the contrary, smaller paychecks for those who do work tend to keep prices down for everyone. When incomes fall below the national average, the cost of living always follow suit.

One more cost-cutting condition: a wave of overbuilding during the easy S&L money era of the 1980s, especially in warm places like Florida, California and Arizona, created a buyer's market in real estate, with rental vacancy rates high. While you might pay $600 a month for an apartment in Dayton, you could be spending $300 for the same quality rental in Daytona Beach. That gives you $300 to put toward groceries and the electric bill. This savings alone is reason enough to pull up stakes from a frigid winter zone. (If you can get the stakes out of the frozen ground.)

This isn't true everywhere in the warm climates. The same pleasant weather that draws ordinary working people quite naturally brings in the big money as well. Places like Palm Beach, Scottsdale or Palm Springs aren't exactly places where you might expect to live on a shoestring. Yet, you'll encounter other places, not too far from these luxury neighborhoods, where prices are reasonable, where living without snow shovels is possible on a restricted budget.

Saving on Utilities

If you live in a cold climate, you don't have to be reminded how much it costs to heat a home in the winter. We've talked to many couples who commonly spend as much as $250 a month on their winter heating bills. Now, in some sections of the country, $250 pays most of the rent for an adequate apartment or a small house, or it can buy groceries for an entire month. As you will see later on, there are inexpensive places to live in this country where air conditioning is non-existent and heating systems are limited to plug-in space heaters. We've interviewed folks who seldom pay more than $50 for utilities year-round, usually far less than that except for January and February. Add that $200 a month savings on utilities to the $300 a month saved on rent, and you are bringing your budget down to the point where you now have money to spend on yourself instead of blowing it on your home and its greedy furnace.

Do You Need Air Conditioning?

Okay, I hear you protesting, "But what about air conditioning in the summer? If I move to a warm climate, I'll have to spend as much to cool my house in the summer as I used to for heating in the winter. Where are the savings?"

Air conditioning is a wonderful invention, something that many people cannot conceive of doing without. Yet, think back a few years—when we were kids—nobody had air conditioning, did they? Yet we survived just fine. Remember when the only air-conditioned building in town was the local movie theater? Remember those signs painted like icicles on the movie marquee that announced "air cooled inside"? In the "good old days," when thermometers topped ninety degrees, our parents used to string a hammock in the shade, relax and sip a cool lemonade or iced tea. Temperatures today haven't changed; unless there is some medical condition to the contrary, you seldom have to turn on the air conditioner.

On the other hand, when below-zero temperatures settle in for the winter, you don't have the option of lighting the furnace or not. If you don't, you die. Winter heating is a matter of life and death, whereas summer air conditioning is a matter of relative comfort.

If you hate the thought of hot summers, yet still want no-frost winters, there are many places in the country (mostly on the West Coast) where air conditioning is unknown. While writing this book, we are living in a California coastal town. None of the houses have air-conditioning because it never gets hot. When temperatures climb into the 80s, our local newspaper reports the event with headlines. On the other hand, in the dead of winter, should temperatures fall low enough for frost to damage our jade plants or fuchsias, you can be sure of more banner headlines. As a matter of fact, we don't even have a furnace; a single gas space heater takes the chill off our large, two-bedroom apartment. You'll find many similar locations along the California, Oregon and Washington coastlines. The best part is, many of these places are very affordable, with among the lowest costs of living in the country and real estate prices approaching rock-bottom.

In my neighborhood, it's shirtsleeve weather in the afternoons, but sweaters after dark year-round. On the other hand, many people love hot weather. They don't want to miss the experience of a real summer—with backyard barbecues, good, honest sunshine that makes a cold drink feel heaven and balmy evenings that invite a dip in the swimming pool. They might not be happy where I live.

The Perfect Climate

Everyone seems to have a different definition of what is a "perfect climate," but the truth is, there is no such thing. Folks in Maine dearly love their summers, but complain that winters are cold and dreary. Their neighbors who retired in Florida adore Miami winters, but complain because summers are too muggy. Hawaii has near-perfect weather, but you'd better take a shopping bag full of money if you expect to stay very long. The nice thing about retirement is you finally have a variety of choices for your weather.

Personally, I consider parts of inland California, Oregon and Washington to have the best overall climate in the nation—sunny summers, with low humidity and relatively free of bugs. (I almost never see a cockroach there.) Winter days require nothing more than a sweater or windbreaker, with little frost or snow—sometimes none all season. To illustrate how ill-prepared some West Coast residents are for cold weather, in the winter of 1990 in Grants Pass, Oregon, an unusual cold snap burst water pipes throughout the area. Grants Pass residents do not customarily protect the pipes from freezing weather because cold snaps are so rare that it isn't worth the bother. But when I lived in Michigan, we wrapped exposed pipes in insulation and used electric warmers—or else.

Cold Weather Robbery

Readers will have little trouble detecting a definite bias in my writing, a bias against winter ice, dirty snow and slush. I fully realize that not everybody is trying to escape snow shovels. Many folks sincerely enjoy winters, with ice fishing, skiing and lovely Christmas card scenery. Therefore, I'll try to be careful not to make this book sound like a chamber of commerce advertisement for Florida or Arizona. But the facts are that cold weather can be very detrimental to your pocketbook—partly because of heating bills and the extra wardrobe required for cold weather, with down jackets, padded boots and long underwear adding to the seasonal expenses. Clothing is a small consideration compared to other items, though, because clothing lasts for many seasons.

One unrecognized cost of cold weather is the subtle destruction of your automobile. Batteries deteriorate quickly in cold weather. Cold-weather starts wear out engine cylinders by dragging moving parts against each other without the benefit of free-flowing oil for lubrication. Antifreeze and snow tires also batter away at the budget. Unlike winter clothing, auto repair and maintenance are ongoing expenses which cannot be put off until next year.

The truly vicious damage comes from the effects of road salt. If you live where roads must be salted to clear away ice and snow you must deduct years from the useful life of your car. Salt destroys steel and body sheet metal faster than termites could ever attack a house! It's interesting to note that in the colder parts of the nation, you rarely see an auto more than ten years old. That's because older cars have long ago dissolved in the salt solutions that slosh around the roads in the winter climates. When you move to a salt-free environment, your car's life expectancy depends on the number of miles you drive, not on the number of winter months you drive. When you need to buy another automobile every three years or so, your shoestring budget gets stretched to the breaking point.

Climate, Exercise and Health

The other way cold weather can be costly is in terms of doctor bills and shortening of your life expectancy. Medical and health experts agree that one of the biggest dangers to retired folks' health is inactivity. Many medical researchers, cardiologists and scientists are coming to the conclusion that exercise is the key factor in health and long life. Exercise, they believe, is far more important than diet.

Unquestionably, people living in warm climates tend to spend more time outdoors. They get out and exercise, doing healthful activities instead of huddling next to the fireplace with eyes glued to the television set. Bicycling, swimming, tennis, daily walks or strolls by the river do wonders for your health and add valuable years to your life. In mild winter climates these are year-round activities, and cost you little or nothing to participate. In cold weather climates folks generally exercise sporadically, if at all.

Some of you will say, "Yes, it would be nice to escape winter, but have you ever tried taking a brisk walk or playing tennis in Florida during August?" They have a point here. Although it is clearly possible to get the exercise out of the way early in the morning or wait until after sundown, many people just cannot stand the muggy humidity of the Southern states and yet don't care to move to the low-humidity Western states.

For some folks, the solution to the climate problem is to become "snowbirds" and enjoy the best of all worlds. Snowbirds are those free spirits who choose to escape winter's anger by flying south for the season. When summer's heat threatens to become oppressive, it's back to a kinder, gentler climate. Snowbirds luxuriate in warm, balmy Phoenix winters and enjoy spring-like summers in

Montana. Those who choose RV retirement usually do exactly that. There is an in-depth discussion of this lifestyle later on in this book.

Finding a Low-Crime Climate

Locating a crime-free area is an important objective for anyone searching for a new retirement home. Unfortunately, as you might guess, there is no such thing as a totally "crime-free" community. There are, however, many "low-crime" areas around the country, and they are relatively simple to locate—particularly if you are rich.

Why rich? Because it turns out that the lowest crime rates in North America are found in the most affluent neighborhoods! I discovered this fact while studying the FBI's crime statistics for cities with populations over 10,000 in the United States. Until then, I had always assumed that most burglaries and robberies would naturally take place in the wealthiest neighborhoods. Not so; the richest neighborhoods generally have exceptionally low rates of burglary, larceny and robbery.

None of the foregoing will comfort those of us who are looking for economical yet safe retirement neighborhoods. However, many low-cost places to retire are just as safe as the expensive spreads such as Palos Verdes or Westchester County. Read on, and we'll explain how to find them.

There's no question the United States is plagued with crime and violence. We're suffering in a way that we didn't dream of back in the 1930s, when the country was in the Depression, unemployment was 20 percent and soup lines were common sights. Yet then folks never bothered to lock their doors at night, and we kids played outside until long after dark. Crime rates then were a fraction of today's.

What's the answer? Some say we need to get tougher on criminals. But how do we do this? We have a higher percentage of our population locked up than any other civilized nation in the world. We can't build prisons fast enough; prisoners are being kicked out of jail before their terms are up in order to make room for more criminals!

Why Some Places Are Safer

The number of police do not determine low-crime areas. Some large, crime-ridden cities have so many cops patrolling the streets that they get in each others' way. Nevertheless, the crime rates remain high. On the other hand, some communities only have part-time police protection, yet burglars are as scarce as honest lawyers. A large police force is usually a response to crime, not an indication of a town's safety.

As a rule, the larger the city, the higher the crime rate. That should be obvious. Yet, even in large cities, you'll find areas of tranquility, sometimes not too far from the problem areas. When checking out a neighborhood for possible retirement, look for mature, low-turnover neighborhoods where residents know each other and the average resident is at or near retirement age.

The age of residents is important. When a low-cost neighborhood is overrun with young people—particularly males between the ages of 15 and 30, most of them under-employed—you are looking at a troubled neighborhood. The FBI reports that 80 percent of all arrests for property crimes or for violent offenses are males, age 20 years or younger. When seeking a rental or a home to buy, cruise the neighborhood and look for teenagers "hanging out" on the street corners. Try to find a neighborhood with older, mature residents; your chances for peace are better there.

Don't make the mistake of automatically connecting unemployment with crime, however. Curiously, some parts of the country with high unemployment rates have far less criminal activity than big cities where work is plentiful. Looking for work does not make a person a criminal.

Drugs and Crime

Why are crime rates sky-high today, yet exceptionally low during the Depression? Why the difference between today's affluent society and the poverty-ridden economy of the Depression? One difference is the ongoing epidemic of hard drugs. In those days, alcohol and tobacco were the drugs of choice—for those who could afford them.

Whether drug addiction is a cause or a symptom of the underlying sickness is hard to say, but we do know that wherever we find high crime rates we also find high drug use. Criminologists estimate that as much as 80 percent of property and violent crimes in our country are drug related—drug addicts pay for their expensive habits through crime. Burglaries, muggings and robberies are the quickest and easiest way to get money. Therefore, when you live in an area of high drug use, your chances of being burglarized are pretty good. Robberies occur 62 times more often in drug-plagued areas. The solution is to look for places where drugs and crime are not out of control.

One way of finding a safe place to live is by studying the local newspapers and seeing how crimes are reported. This can tell you a lot about how safe a town is by the importance accorded various crimes. When murder, robberies and burglaries are reported routinely or not at all, you can be sure this is a high-crime-rate area. But when a bicycle theft makes headlines, you've found a safe community.

For example, not long ago, when I was visiting New York City, I noticed a small article in the New York Times with a headline that read: "Two Shot Dead and Three Hurt after Collision." The killings occurred in Manhattan after a fender-bender at an intersection. Apparently the problem started when someone in the crowd pointed out that one of the cars was blocking traffic. This incensed the driver, so he pulled a gun and opened fire on the crowd of bystanders. Two dead, three wounded. If a horrible thing like this happened in most parts of the world, headlines would have screamed the event on front pages across every newspaper in the country. Yet, in New York City a crime of this magnitude only rated a one-column story on the corner of page 23—and only then because more than one individual was murdered. Had it only been one person killed, it may not have made the news at all.

You can't blame the newspaper; murders are so common in that city that if all of them were reported on the front page there wouldn't be room for other news. As a matter of fact, that same article reported that this double murder was just one of three incidents that night involving automobiles and gunfire which ended in death. Don't you find this shocking? Although at least two other humans had been shot to death after traffic accidents that same night, the events were so unremarkable that they only rated a one-sentence announcement on page 23! The victims weren't newsworthy enough to have their names published, so their murders were reported as casually as a stock market report in my hometown newspaper.

Therefore, if murders and rapes are reported on page 23, if at all, you can presuppose violent crime to be epidemic. On the other hand, if a burglary makes page one headlines, then burglaries can't be all that common. If a newspaper publishes a detailed police log, read it over carefully. In town where police are mostly involved in cases such as rescuing a cat from Mrs. Smith's tree or recovering a bicycle stolen from Jimmy Jones' front yard, crime probably isn't exactly out of control.

Having said that, I have to point out a contradiction. In tourist-oriented communities, a weekly police log can be deceiving. I have a friend who is a police officer in a prime tourist area, and he complains that serious crimes are sometimes not reported in the local newspaper. The police chief and city officials want to present a calm and peaceful front so as not to scare away tourists or potential buyers of resort property. The newspaper reporter is given a list of crimes for the week, but only those the police chief wants known. In other words, read between the lines if it's a tourist-oriented area you are considering.

Safety Tips

Your local office on aging and police department can help you make your home or apartment more secure. In most communities these organizations work together to publish educational materials about crime prevention and sponsor crime prevention projects.

Often your police department will be happy to send a police officer to your home to check on your home security and make suggestions for your safety. Some of the more common security recommendations:
- Always lock your garage, even if you are at home or just step out briefly.
- When you are out of the house, lock your windows as well as your doors.
- Cut back bushes near doors and windows.
- Install dead-bolt locks and night chains.
- Install and use a peephole.
- Keep outside areas well-illuminated.
- Keep valuable personal property in a safe deposit box rather than at home.
- Do not keep large amounts of cash in the house.
- Do not hide an extra set of keys to your home in obvious places, such as under the doormat, on the ledge above your door, in a planter box, or mailbox.

If you go away on a trip:
- Use timers to keep lights on inside and outside the house in the evening.
- Stop mail and newspaper deliveries, and ask a neighbor to pick up circulars and packages from your driveway.
- Hide your empty garbage cans.
- Arrange for someone to maintain your yard.
- Turn your telephone bell down.

FBI Statistics

For serious research as to an area's crime status, you can visit your local library and ask for a copy of the latest FBI Uniform Crime Report. This publication lists all towns with populations over 10,000 and ranks them as to the various types of crimes. The list is broken down into the types of crime: murder, forcible rape, robbery, aggravated assault, burglary, larceny-theft and automobile theft. But don't hang your hat on statistics; even small towns can be crime ridden and most big cities have safe neighborhoods.

Chapter Eight

Mobile Home Living

Some folks, when they near retirement, begin thinking of selling their home and "drawing in their horns" by buying a mobile home. Many consider this an ideal way to live in comfort, convenience and on a minimum amount of money. Approximately four million mobile homes in the United States house about eight-and-a-half million people, most of whom are retired. Many parks are exclusively inhabited by retired folks. Those who have chosen the mobile home lifestyle point out that this is one option for home ownership without the high investment and real estate taxes that go with most property. As one couple said, "It costs us only $100 a month to live in our own home. And that includes water, garbage and sewer. We don't pay property tax; we buy a license plate."

Not all mobile home parks are inexpensive, of course; some charge as much as or more than apartment rentals in the same neighborhood. Generally, space rents depend upon the facilities and scarcity of mobile home spaces in the locality.

The least expensive place we found was in the California desert near the Salton Sea. It was an eight-foot-wide, 32-foot-long Vagabond (1952 vintage) for $800, with space rent a mere $50 a month. (You probably wouldn't want to live there.) The most expensive mobile home housing we've heard of was a used 1,000-square-foot, metal-sided home priced at $150,000, with a space rent of $1,180 per month. (You probably wouldn't want to live there, either—not on a shoestring.)

Mobility

Mobile homes today are anything but mobile. Most are so wide and so long that only specialized companies attempt to move or install them. The manufacturers are trying to change the term to "manufactured" homes, yet the buyers insist on the term "mobile." Curiously, many people still refer to mobile homes as "coaches," a real artifact of early trailer living.

Once installed on a site—joined together into three- and four-bedroom units complete with everything but a basement swimming pool—they are permanently in place. Then how did they get the name "mobile"? It started after World War II when they actually were mobile—only eight feet wide and rarely more than 35 feet long. Because of a severe post-war housing shortage, hundreds of thousands of house trailers were built, and families used them to travel to job locations and as homes. Construction workers found house trailers indispensable; they were easily towed behind the family car, and they could be placed near, or sometimes on, the job site. Although they were the size of today's recreational vehicles, their purpose was not recreation, but housing.

But many families who lived in these temporary housing units felt embarrassed at the concept of "house trailer." They remembered the days when depression-bruised families were forced to live in dilapidated house trailers because of economic straits rather than as a temporary convenience. Therefore, to put a more positive spin on the situation, house trailers became known as "mobile homes."

For Retirement

Some upscale mobile home parks offer amenities such as Olympic-sized swimming pools, hot tubs, jacuzzis, tennis courts, spacious clubhouses and just about everything you expect to find in expensive apartments or luxury condos. You don't have to worry about landscaping or maintenance of anything but your own small plot of ground.

Sometimes, even individual landscaping chores are taken care of by the park management. And, because mobile home parks are frequently enclosed by fences, with limited outside access, they are unusually safe. Some of the more expensive parks are totally closed, with security guards posted at the entrances around the clock. In any case, because the homes are close together, and because residents know each other far better than in traditional neighborhoods, criminal activities are rather quickly noted.

The standard width of a mobile home today is 12 feet, with lengths up to 70 feet. Some are even 14 feet wide. When two of these units are joined together, forming a "double-wide," you end up with a good-size home. The square footage is often larger than your original home. If you've ever visited one of the expensively furnished display models at your local mobile home sales lot, you've probably been dazzled at the luxury and spaciousness.

What does it cost to live in a mobile home? That's like asking what it costs to live in a house; it all depends on the cost of the house and the neighborhood. We've seen acceptable park spaces renting for as little as $75 a month, and others for much, much more.

For example: we looked at a park near Sarasota, Florida, that featured a landscaped lakefront, a beautiful clubhouse and tennis courts, plus the inevitable swimming pool—for around $215 a month. Used two-bedroom mobile homes were priced at $14,000 to $21,000, with new units starting at $29,000. A social director arranged a full schedule of activities for the park residents. We talked to a retired couple who recently purchased a double-wide home in the park. "We sold our place in Michigan for $50,000 clear," said the husband, "and we considered putting the money into a condo in Sarasota. It was nice—a clubhouse, swimming pool and bike paths. But the monthly maintenance fee was almost what we pay for rent here." His wife added, "So we bought this place for $18,000. It has everything the condo had, and now we have over $30,000 to invest for income."

Another park, just a few miles away, was full of older units, many 10 to 20 years old, more closely spaced. The major facility was the laundry room—which traditionally serves each park as a major place to meet, socialize and exchange gossip. According to residents, all of whom were retired, there was a satisfactory level of social activity, organized by residents on an informal basis rather than by the park management. It was quite pleasant and peaceful, with mature trees for shade. A few homes displayed "for sale" signs, including a single-wide, one-bedroom place for under $8,000. Park rent was $155 a month. Space rent further out in the country was even less expensive, as low as $80 a month, according to some park managers.

It's interesting to note that many parks—particularly the higher-quality ones—prohibit posting "for sale" signs on the homes. Thus, you might drive through a park and gather the impression that there is nothing for sale. When you cannot find signs, simply inquire at the park manager's office. Partly this rule is to keep things uncluttered by signs and advertisements, but part of it is also the management's desire to filter out undesirable tenants they do not want to buy into the park.

Purchase Prices

Prices vary widely, depending on the newness of the mobile home, the condition of the park and, most of all, the scarcity of park spaces in the area. Bear in mind, you are paying for the location rather than the actual value of the home. A mobile home located in a city where spaces are scarce could sell for $30,000, whereas the identical make and year—located in a town where mobile home lot vacancies are plentiful—might be worth only $5,000. Mobile home salesmen are quick to claim that this difference in value is appreciation. Appreciation has nothing to do with it; the extra money simply reflects the scarcity of park spaces. When land is valuable, fewer entrepreneurs are willing to devote it to mobile home parks unless there is a good return on the investment. That's why in smaller towns, where land is cheaper, mobile home prices and park rents are far less.

We recently looked at a 14'x70', two-bedroom, two-bath mobile, with new appliances and a 10'x12' storage shed, situated on a large fenced lot for $7,800. In a similar park in a large city the unit would sell for closer to $40,000. Another home, this one an older 10'x55' with an expanded living room, also two-bedroom, but with just one bath, was listed at $3,500, but the owner hinted he would take much less on a cash sale. Had this been in a nice park and in a tighter rental market, it would probably sell for at least $15,000. Remember, the difference in selling price is due to scarcity of land, not the value of the mobile home. The fact is, mobile homes depreciate, just like automobiles. Don't let any salesman tell you differently.

Pitfalls for Mobile Home Buyers

It's true: a mobile home can be an excellent way of cutting back on living costs. On the other hand, if you're not careful, it could turn out to be a seriously costly and risky investment. Some hazards lurk out there to trip up unwary buyers. A few missteps, and mobile home living becomes far more expensive than owning a conventional home. Some problems can be avoided if you can keep from being blinded by the beautiful furnishings or a dealer's glowing sales pitch. That's only part of it; other important conditions need close investigation.

For one thing, I personally would never purchase a new unit and have it set up in a park. It makes much more sense to buy one already in place, with all the costs known—landscaping, carport, storage shed, and so forth—all in place and ready to use. If the unit is used, so much the better because, despite what a salesman might tell you, mobile homes do not appreciate in price like ordinary real estate does. They depreciate. The older the unit, the less you should consider paying. Let's examine why.

Although you own your mobile home, the land it's sitting on belongs to someone else. Obviously, you are simply renting a patch of land from month to month. A problem arises when the park is in an area of rapid development.

You could suddenly find that the owner of the property wants to kick everybody off and sell the land for a shopping mall. The land has become too valuable to be kept as a mobile home park. This happens all too frequently. When a developer offers big bucks, the park owner can easily succumb to the temptation to become wealthy in a hurry instead of counting on your monthly rent.

A situation like this is much more serious than simply being the annoyance of having to move your home to another location. Moving one of these so-called "mobile" homes is not a job to be taken lightly. You are at the mercy of professionals who may take full advantage of your plight. That's bad enough, but when all mobile home parks in the area are full, and there is no place to move, your home becomes all but worthless. Even when spaces are available, many parks refuse to accept any unit that is over five years old. The better parks only accept brand-new mobile homes. Worse yet, some parks only accept homes they sell themselves. An out-of-town dealer might offer you a pittance for your unit; he will haul it to some other part of the state where park spaces are abundant.

Scope out the mobile home park situation in the area thoroughly before making any decisions. Talk to park residents where you are thinking of buying. Go to the laundry room and start asking questions. This is easy to do, because the laundry room is not only the nerve center of a mobile home park, but a place where folks are unusually friendly and talkative. While waiting for their clothes to dry, they happily talk each other's ears to stubs. Ask residents if they have worries about the park's future.

If you ask about the park's management or the owner, be prepared to hear all the good and bad things about living there. Too often park managers, lowly paid and spiteful, find a sense of power in their new jobs and can become virtual Napoleons. I know of one instance when a new manager forced everyone to get rid of all landscaping shrubs alongside their mobile homes by treating the soil with something like Agent Orange and covering the sterile ground with decorative white rock. "If you don't like it, you can just move," he warned. The next manager decreed that the white rock had to go and grass and shrubs be replanted in the now-dead soil—or else. You don't need a situation where tenants are continually skirmishing with management. An aware and caring park ownership rarely hires this kind of employee.

Check the local classifieds and see if mobile home spaces are listed in the "for rent" columns. If they are, you can assume that park openings are plentiful. Look at the "mobile homes for sale" columns to check prices and visit the parks to see where you might move if you have to. Do this even if you are buying a new unit. You never know.

Another consideration is that a scarcity of mobile home spaces usually cause space rents to escalate far beyond the rate of inflation. My wife and I lived in a mobile home park in San Jose, California, for several years. When we moved in, our space rent was a delightfully low $95 a month. Seven years later, when we moved out, the rent was $395! However, that was not the reason we sold our mobile home; it was because of the dreaded "15-year rule."

The 15-Year Rule

This is the biggest zinger of all. Many mobile home parks around the nation try to maintain a spiffy image by continually upgrading the homes in their developments. Replacing older units with glitzy new models keeps the park looking new, thus justifying higher rental costs. Managers seldom go around evicting older units, but when possible they invoke a "15-year rule." That is, whenever a mobile home more than 15 years old is sold, it must be removed from the park. If spaces are at a premium in the area, the mobile home becomes practically unmarketable. Most buyers of used mobile homes want a place to live in, not a mobile home that they have to move. In this type of situation, depreciation accelerates rapidly and your investment fades quickly as your unit approaches the magic 15-year limit. Some parks have a 20-year limit, but the end results are the same.

Therefore, it's essential to know management's policy on older homes, particularly if you are thinking about saving money and purchasing one that is 13 or 14 years old. Some states and cities have laws prohibiting this age discrimination (Florida, for one). A mobile home there can only be evicted for unsafe or unsightly conditions. That's not to say that some park managers won't look for ways to get rid of older mobile homes one way or another. So, if a mobile home unit is kept in good condition, one 15 or 20 years old can be an excellent buy, provided it isn't in danger of eviction.

A final caution is against moving into a "family" park—particularly one of the older, run-down parks. Young, low-income families who live in these parks (often on welfare) will crowd into a small trailer with three or four youngsters. Keeping the kids outside, playing in your yard, is the only way the parents get any peace and quiet. Too often they exert no control nor show any serious concern over their offspring's behavior. When you have a gaggle of kids trooping through a park in search of entertainment, you not only have noise, but you are bound to have vandalism, even if accidental. Youngsters cease to be cute when they start unplugging your electricity, drawing pictures on your automobile or picking your flowers to take home to mommy. (All of these happened to friends of mine who lived in family mobile home parks.) Adult parks are customarily quiet, and chances are better that you and your neighbors will have something in common.

Having said all of these negative things about mobile home buying, let me say that of all the retired folks we've interviewed, some of the happiest are those living this lifestyle. It's economical and practically worry-free, as long as you keep your eyes open and heed some of the advice herewith.

Buying Your Own Lot

Some mobile home developments sell lots rather than simply renting them. This is usually a package deal; they sell you a mobile home as well as the land. One park we visited in Texas offered a $38,900 package (including taxes and fees) for a good-size lot and a two-bedroom mobile home with carport, utility room and a screen room. The development had a 24-hour guarded gate, a swimming pool and tennis courts.

When buying into a development, make sure you actually hold title to the land and not just a revocable lease. A good salesman can make a lease sound exactly like an iron-clad deed. Also be aware that even though you own the lot, you will be liable for monthly maintenance and membership fees. These could be as high as rent in a similar-quality park.

Rock-Bottom Mobile Home Living

Many of those older, eight-foot-wide units that were popular before the wider ones came into vogue are still around and still in livable condition. In their heyday, they were built for full-time living instead of just summer vacations like most travel trailers today. They were solidly built, sometimes of galvanized steel, and extremely well insulated. Instead of small space heaters, they usually have oil or gas furnaces with forced-air heat. Because they have only a small interior space to heat in the winter or to air condition in the summer, utility bills are almost a joke. The ones that survive make excellent, inexpensive living quarters, and if push comes to shove, they can be moved easily. A pickup or an old Cadillac with a good equalizer hitch can zip them away—no problem—with no special permits or "wide load" warnings front and rear required.

Because these survivors are old-fashioned and clumsy-looking, with birch-finished interiors instead of today's plastic and simulated-wood panels, these older units often go for incredibly low prices. You'll not find them in newer mobile home parks because they've long since been kicked out, to "upgrade" the park. Yet, they make comfortable living quarters and have surprisingly efficient interiors for storage and everyday living. Beds are usually built in, as is the living room furniture, therefore you won't have to buy furnishings. You do need to inspect these units carefully for water damage and dry rot, though, and you must make sure the undercarriage is sturdy (not rusted through).

The next step up from the eight-footer is the ten-foot wide mobile home. These are more spacious and often have eight-foot expansion rooms which make the living rooms or bedrooms a spacious 18 feet wide. When both living room and bedroom are expanded, it's called a "double expando." You don't feel as if you are in a trailer when in one of these. They sell for a bit more than the older units, but far less than the newer 12-footers.

An Affordable Winter Home

These older, inexpensive mobiles are ideal for summer homes in the mountains or winter retreats for escaping freezing weather and outrageous utility bills. For example: we looked at one park in Yuma, Arizona, that catered exclusively to retired folks who live elsewhere, but enjoy the warm Arizona sunshine for the winter. Almost all units were "8-wides."

Since the landscaping uses natural desert plants, there is virtually no upkeep problem for the winter residents. Residents pay $180 a month rent (including electricity, water and garbage) while they stay in their winter mobile homes, and then $50 a month through the summer when the place is abandoned except for the park owners. It's a good deal for the park owners, because for half the year they don't have to bother with tenants, and it works out well for the winter residents because they don't have to pull an RV back and forth every season and then pay $50 a month for RV storage back home. Two of these units were for sale, one for about $8,000 and one for $6,000.

The winter visitors start arriving in Arizona about the middle of November. When they have a quorum at the clubhouse, they elect officers for the season, appoint committee members and decide on a calendar of events. A recent calendar included trips to nearby Mexico, Las Vegas and Disneyland. Dances, potlucks and card games completed the social schedule.

"We can't afford to stay home," one lady said. "In our Wyoming home, we would be spending at least $250 a month to heat our place. And when the north wind blows, nothing will keep the house warm." She was wearing shorts and a halter as she rode a bicycle around the park. Her husband was out playing golf.

We asked what she figured for a budget during the winter months. She replied, "With $180 for rent, about $250 for food, $100 for entertainment and $200 for miscellaneous, we manage everything on my husband's Social Security."

Try Before You Buy?

Ordinarily, I'd advise you to rent before deciding to buy. However, for mobile homes, this usually turns out to be impractical. That's because all but the most humble (sometimes sleazy) parks strictly prohibit residents from renting out their mobile homes. This is an almost universal rule: no rentals. Places where renting is permitted are generally places you wouldn't want to live, anyway. This isn't always true, of course, but don't count on finding anything you might like.

We have found one exception to the no-rental policy. It's an interesting concept in mobile home living—one we've seen in a few Florida parks and which may possibly be available elsewhere. It's called a "try before you buy" plan. A park near the town of Hudson, Florida, is an example of this. Average-looking, well-kept and nicely landscaped—but without a golf course or lake—this park has a limited number of two-bedroom, furnished mobile homes for lease. The minimum stay is three months, the maximum six months. The manager of the park told us, "We don't make money on these leases, but after folks spend a month or two here, getting acquainted, they usually buy. This is our best sales producer."

The manager pointed out that this is an excellent way to discover three things about yourself. First, you will find out whether or not you like Florida well enough to retire there. Second, you will learn whether you like that particular part of Florida. And third, you will discover whether you like mobile home living well enough to retire in one. The monthly charges are stiff, starting at $500, but this includes linens, dishes and cooking utensils, unlimited use of the clubhouse and pool, plus lawn maintenance.

Instant Housing

For inexpensive, quick housing on your own land, you can't beat a mobile home. All it takes is someone to move it onto your lot, and you have plumbing, electricity and a comfortable place to live. By the way, the best way to buy a mobile home for your property is to look for one of those distress sales mentioned earlier, one of the 15-year-rule disasters which must be moved at any price. When a mobile must be moved, you can cut the asking price drastically.

You will, of course, need to check local regulations very carefully before placing a mobile on your lot. Many localities absolutely prohibit them on private land. In addition, you need to investigate several other things, particularly if you plan on buying property out in the country. The following items must be considered.

1. Are electricity and telephone services available? If you have to pay to install telephone and power poles several miles to your place, you might end up paying more for that than the cost of the land and mobile home combined.

2. A good water supply is essential; if city water isn't connected to the property, you'll need to know how much it will cost to bring it in. The alternative is a well, which could be expensive, depending upon the locality. Even if a well is possible, you need to be assured that the water is drinkable. I have a friend who spent several thousand dollars drilling a well through layers of hard rock, only to find the water tastes like sulfur and smells like rotten eggs. Makes for unpleasant showers, to say the least.

3. If a city sewer hookup isn't in the picture, you'll likely need a permit for a septic system. Sometimes this is

impossible to obtain. Percolation tests may be required, and if your property can't qualify, you could end up using the bathroom at the nearest filling station. If your luck is really bad, it will be a pay toilet, so keep a plentiful supply of coins on hand.

4. If your land is truly out in the country, you must be sure you have access easements across other people's property to reach your land. This is not only important for a road or driveway, but for stringing power and telephone lines as well. If your neighbors are not the friendly type, the only way to reach your property could be by parachute.

5. Check your deed for timber and mineral rights. Usually these aren't important, but if your land is in a mining or timber-harvesting area—as are parts of the Ozarks— you could find bulldozers strip-mining your front yard or chain saws rearranging the landscaping.

Buying a Mobile Home and Land

The total investment in a mobile home on private land can be quite minimal, but it does entail a bit of work to get set up. Sometimes the obstacles are much more formidable than meet the eye. Frankly, I believe it's better to let someone else do the work; I'd prefer to buy something already set up and ready for occupancy.

During our research travels, we found exceptional buys in mobile homes on their own lots. For example: How does $10,000 sound for a double-wide, two-bedroom unit sitting on ten acres of wooded lands? Or a single-wide on a riverside lot for $9,000? These are common prices to be found in the Ozarks area of Missouri, Arkansas and Oklahoma. One lovely place was a five-minute drive from a boat ramp on Lake Tanycomo. The double-wide mobile home was set back among a growth of pine trees, almost hidden from the road, and surrounded by over ten acres of wooded solitude—with an asking price of $17,000. Of all the landed mobile home setups we've seen, the Ozarks offer the best bargains.

It should go without saying that you need to be positive that country living is what you really want. If you crave fishing, hunting and communing with the outdoors, while your spouse cannot stand the sight of dead catfish or the thought of doing without HBO on cable TV, it may be time to talk about a compromise place to retire.

Chapter Nine

College Town Retirement

Have you ever noticed something special about small college towns? Life moves at a different pace—relaxed, yet filled with stimulating activities and possibilities. Something's always happening. An exhilarating feeling of progress and excitement permeates the air.

A university not only influences the intellectual atmosphere, but indirectly affects the business, entertainment and dining traditions as well. A university lures intellectuals from all over the world, creating an air of sophistication unknown in most towns of moderate size. Yet, when you stroll along a downtown street, strangers are likely to nod and say "hello" as they pass. After all, this is not just a small town, it's a college town. Most people are connected with the university in one way or another. We're all neighbors.

Today, one of the more interesting trends in retirement is a movement toward relocation in college towns. Retirees find inexpensive access to cultural events, low crime, good health-care facilities and a heart-warming mix of age groups. Responding to this interest, and seeing the advantages of money-spending retirees moving to the area, universities make it easy for senior citizens to register and attend classes. Special programs are offered, oriented toward mature students. Classes feature topics like "Today's Best-Selling Novelists" and "Introduction to Computers."

A few months ago, while interviewing John Leslie—the mayor of Oxford, Mississippi—I commented on the old-fashioned charm of the downtown square. Like many university communities, Oxford's central business district manages to combine yesterday's grace with tasteful, modern convenience. A half-dozen excellent restaurants, a nationally-celebrated bookstore, boutiques and art galleries join a 150-year-old furniture store and a wide variety of other traditional establishments.

Mayor Leslie agreed, saying, "When you combine a large number of university students with a large number of retired folks, you just naturally get a demand for a higher level of services, nicer shopping facilities and better restaurants." And, I must add, at reasonable costs. Neither students nor retirees tend to be overburdened with money, and they appreciate quality at affordable prices.

College town retirement is one of those choices worth examining closely. Living costs are often no higher than in similar-sized towns in the area. Since as many as half of the community's residents are non-working students, there's not a lot of extra money bidding up rentals and real estate costs. There is one economic downside to retirement in a college town: vigorous competition for part-time work. Unless you have a special skill or can do some teaching, you may have plenty of spare time to enjoy retirement and volunteer jobs.

Even if you have no intention of going back to school, you'll discover many benefits in retiring in a university setting. Most institutions provide the community at large with a wide selection of social and cultural activities. You don't have to be a registered student to attend lectures and speeches (often free) given by famous scientists, politicians, visiting artists and other well-known personalities. Concerts, ranging from Beethoven to boogie-woogie, are presented by guest artists as well as the university's music department. Stage plays, from Broadway musicals to Shakespeare, are produced by the drama department, with season tickets often less than a single performance at a New York theater. Some schools make special provisions to allow seniors to use their recreational facilities. Art exhibits, panel discussions and a well-stocked library are often available to the public. (You can't check out library books or magazines, but you're usually free to browse the stacks.)

Every college town has at least one large bookstore where you'll enjoy one or two free events each week. You'll have the opportunity of meeting a best-selling author and listening to her discuss her latest work. In some bookstores, you can sip a coffee and listen to a string quartet while you browse. Because of a high level of sophistication, most college towns support bars and restaurants that feature entertainment, often well-known talent. Ordinary towns nearby seldom have this. Throughout the Southern states, where some of the more delightful college towns are located, "local option" has "dried up" surrounding counties, but most college towns have managed to reject the notion of prohibition.

You don't have to go back to school, but as long as you're retiring in a college town, why not give continuing education a try? More and more, dynamic seniors with active lifestyles are enjoying the pleasant, invigorating mental exercise of part-time classes. And this time around, they sign up for subjects they want to study, rather than what's required to get a degree!

Scientific research shows that as we age, we don't necessarily lose our capacity to learn. Furthermore, the common belief that memory fades with each passing year is simply not true. Numerous psychological experiments prove that those who regularly exercise their minds hold up quite well, thank you.

More than two-thirds of all colleges and universities offer reduced rates or even free tuition to older citizens. Many communities have special centers, schools and programs tailored to older adults' needs. You won't feel like the proverbial sore thumb in a setting where many students are your age or older.

Nervous about going back to school? Never been in a college classroom? Don't worry, for a mature adult it's a snap. Most professors are much closer to your age than to the other students. They'll tend to treat you as an equal, while talking down to younger students. Most schools allow you to audit a course, which means you take the class but don't have to worry about tests, finals or term papers. You get the benefits and fun from the course without the tension.

If a university classroom seems a bit much for your ambitions, then try adult ed classes. You'll find a broad assortment of offerings, everything from philosophy to auto repair. The bonus is that in many college towns, you'll find that the adult ed instructor is also a university professor, moonlighting for extra money or simply because he enjoys sharing his special expertise.

University level or adult ed, it doesn't matter. You'll find yourself amidst a group of lively, interesting people—the kind you would like for friends.

University Retirement Sampler

Following are some places I particularly like, towns where folks retire primarily because of the university setting. Of course, many other college towns throughout the nation offer everything that my favorites do. Doing your own investigation could turn up a setting that better suits your taste in climate, recreation and location. You can take advantage of continuing education just about anywhere you choose to retire. For example, most small cities without a university usually have two-year community colleges. It's just that in some towns, the university is the centerpiece of local attention, the focus of social and cultural activities. This creates a situation where everyone can participate in the excitement generated by the university. The following places are my personal favorites:

Oxford, Mississippi. Stately antebellum mansions, enormous magnolia trees, live oaks and flowers in profusion, an ancient courthouse and statue of a Confederate soldier, all of these combine to make Oxford a model of a gracious Old-Southern university town. This is my all-time favorite college town. A city of 20,000 (half of them students), Oxford is large enough to provide quality services, but small enough that you'll meet friends just about every time you go to the supermarket or walk to the library.

Housing costs are as low as any quality location you'll find in the South, one of the many attractions that draw retirees from all sections of the country. A nice mixture of "Yankees" and deep-South natives adds spice to the flavor of retiring here; if you're not from the South, you won't be a stranger here. The 140-year-old university also lures intellectuals from all over the world, creating an air of sophistication unknown in most isolated Southern towns. Retirees find Oxford a wonderful place for education; anyone over the age of 55 can take three hours of classes tuition-free per semester and can audit as many classes as they care to.

Columbia, Missouri. This is more than a "college town"; it's more properly called a "university city." Several times the size of Oxford—with a population of 70,000—Columbia blends the sophistication of a small city with an exciting academic environment. Instead of just one university, three well-known institutions of higher learning make education a major industry here. Some programs offer free tuition in return for volunteer work after graduation. Kansas City and St. Louis are two-hour interstate drives in either direction for those who can't live without major league sports or other amenities of big-city life.

Making the decision to retire in Columbia is made easier by a unique chamber of commerce program. Retiree volunteers greet visitors and take them on a "windshield tour" of the city. They drive you through neighborhoods ranging from economical to deluxe, past the town's colleges, golf courses and hospitals.

Ashland, Oregon. Couples with mixed interests, who want more than intellectual stimulation, might check out Ashland. Set in southern Oregon's gently rolling hills, Ashland is an excellent retirement choice for outdoorsy, sports-oriented people. Great hunting, fishing and skiing are available in the nearby Cascade Range, with crystal-clear rivers teeming with world-class salmon and steelhead trout. Whitewater rafting on the wild and scenic Rogue River draws adventurers from all over the country. One of the best climates in the nation makes outdoor sports enjoyable year-round; Ashland's 20 inches of yearly rain is a third to half that of most popular Midwest and Southern cities, so it's wonderfully sunny here most of the year.

Yet, Ashland also offers all the usual cultural amenities of a small college town and more. Its widely-renowned Shakespeare festival draws thousands every summer, and year-round community involvement in the college's activities keeps retirement interesting. A charming downtown offers excellent restaurants and shopping. As a final incentive, real estate costs are typical Oregon, ranging between cheap and affordable.

Auburn-Opelika, Alabama. Eastern Alabama's rolling hills and forests provide a good setting for the adjoining towns of Auburn and Opelika, with a combined population of 57,000. Low property taxes are a bonus. Centered around Auburn University, this area draws a diverse mixture of retirees from all over the nation. In fact, a third of all Auburn-Opelika residents come from other states.

In addition to the university, there's a two-year school with about 1,400 students and Opelika State Technical School with extended day programs. Because of the university's top medical school and the East Alabama Medical Center, health care here is superior. Nearby Fort Benning, Georgia, has medical facilities for military retirees, as well as a commissary and post exchange.

One of the famous Robert Trent Jones Golf Trail courses is located here, offering top country-club quality at public golf fees. Great fishing is enjoyed at any number of sparkling lakes around the countryside. The climate here is mild, with a brief winter, early spring and late fall.

Gainesville, Florida. Home of the University of Florida, Gainesville is a culturally stimulating city of 90,000 inhabitants, in a state which is famous for its culturally unstimulating cities. It doesn't look like Florida, either. Were it not for an occasional palm tree, Gainesville could be easily mistaken for a college town anywhere in the Midwest. Old-fashioned residential areas with tree-shaded streets justify Gainesville's official nickname, "The Tree City."

You needn't be a student to participate in the many activities connected with the university. A cultural complex with museums of art and natural history and a performing arts center serve the public at large. There is also an excellent two-year college that accepts students over 60 tuition-free under most circumstances. The extensive curriculum covers classes like dog training, computers and antique collecting.

If a town of 90,000 is too large for you, nearby High Springs and Archer are a 15-minute drive away. Housing costs less here and small farms are affordable.

For outdoors people, there's plenty to do. A dozen nearby lakes invite anglers. Golf and tennis facilities abound, and beach fun at either the Gulf or the Atlantic is a short drive away. The closest saltwater fishing is in Cedar Key, a 49-mile drive to the Gulf.

Chico, California. Only a 20-minute drive from tree-covered mountains, fishing and hunting, and just a little further to winter skiing, Chico is the site of a California State University. This is a typical Sacramento valley town, with live oaks and huge ash trees shading quiet streets on topography as flat as a table. The thing that lifts Chico above most small, agriculturally centered valley towns is its university and vibrant academic timbre. Like all California State Universities, Chico State encourages senior citizen participation with free and reduced tuition rates. Cultural events, such as concerts, plays, lectures and foreign films, are plentiful and, more often than not, free.

Chico weather, as in all Sacramento River valley towns, is both a blessing and a drawback, depending on your opinion of how hot summers should be. You can find days on end with temperatures in the 100-degree range. Balance that against the warm, seldom-frosty winter days with almost no snow, and Chico's weather comes out a winner. After all, when the summer gets going, that's the time for you to head for the nearby mountains for a picnic beside a cool stream or a day's prospecting and panning for gold in the Feather River.

Tuition Breaks

Many states have legislation granting free or reduced tuition to senior citizens. Here's a list of the states and their policies. Some states are considering liberalizing these regulations, so check locally for up-to-date facts. The information comes from a report by the U.S. Senate Special Committee on Aging.

Alabama: Most of Alabama's colleges and universities offer free or reduced tuition to residents 60 or over. Some private schools offer tuition discounts, special classes, and access to recreation and cultural programs for retirees.

Arkansas: State schools waive general student fees for credit courses to persons age 60 and older on a space available basis. State vocational and technical schools also waive fees.

California: Depending upon space, many state colleges waive application and regular-session registration fees for regular credit courses to persons age 60 or older.

District of Columbia: The University of the District of Columbia waives tuition for students age 60 or older in courses for credit or audit.

Florida: Waives application, course registration and related fees at state universities on a space-available basis to residents age 60 or older.

Georgia: Waives fees for courses scheduled for resident credit to persons age 62 and older on a space-available basis.

Hawaii: Waives tuition or fees for credit classes at the University of Hawaii to persons age 60 or older, on a space-available basis.

Kentucky: Waives all tuition and fees at state-supported institutions of higher learning to any resident age 65 and older, on a space-available basis.

Louisiana: Waives tuition and registration fees at public colleges and universities to any person age 60 or older. Also reduces textbook costs by 50 percent.

Maryland: Waives tuition to the University of Maryland system for up to three courses per term to any retired person age 60 or older, on a space-available basis. Also waives tuition to community colleges to residents age 60 or older.

Mississippi: Waives tuition to residents 55 and older for one credit class per semester, with unlimited auditing, on a space-available basis.

Nevada: Waives registration fee for credit or audit in any course to persons age 62 and older.

New Mexico: Institutions may reduce tuition fees to $5 per credit hour for up to six hours per semester to residents age 65 or older, on a space-available basis.

North Carolina: Waives tuition at colleges and universities to residents age 65 or older who attend classes for credit or non-credit, on a space-available basis.

South Carolina: Waives tuition at any public college or university for credit or non-credit classes to residents age 60 or older, on a space-available basis.

Tennessee: Waives tuition and registration fees at public colleges and universities for credit or audit to residents age 65 and older, on a space-available basis.

Texas: State-supported schools may waive tuition for persons age 65 or older to audit any course, on a space-available basis.

Utah: Waives tuition at institutions of higher learning to residents age 62 or older, on a space-available basis.

Virginia: Waives tuition for auditing courses at any state institution of higher education to residents age 60 or older, on a space-available basis, with an income limit of $10,000.

Washington: State universities and community colleges may waive tuition to residents age 60 or older enrolled for credit, on a space-available basis.

Chapter Ten

RVs and Retirement

Of all the lifestyles open to low-income retirees, few can accommodate a shoestring budget as well as recreational vehicle retirement does. This presumes, of course, that your motorhome, trailer or camper is paid for or that you aren't facing stiff monthly payments.

If you've ever owned an RV, chances are you've fantasized about how it might be to actually live in your rig instead of merely vacationing. You imagine yourself taking off and never landing, following the seasons, catering to your whims, happy as a seagull soaring in the breeze. It's an exciting, awesome idea. You totally change your old lifestyle, rent out the house, put things in storage and set out with no particular destination in mind! The best part is, for those searching for low-cost retirement, RV living can fill the bill. It depends on how you go about it, of course.

This enthusiasm over RV living is comparatively new. Years ago, before the phenomenal growth of the recreational vehicle industry, RVs were primarily used for weekends and summer vacations. Travel trailers were rarely self-contained (although some models had flush toilets which needed to be hooked to sewer connections before they could be used). Pickup trucks with cab-over campers were the forerunners of today's luxury motorhomes. Those few folks who traveled full time in cramped little trailers were considered to be gypsies, eccentrics or adventurers. Living in the back of a pickup was the sign of a loser.

Times have changed, and RVs have changed along with the times. Today, uncounted thousands of retired folks spend months at a time in fifth-wheels, motorhomes and deluxe cab-overs. If you still believe RVs are for gypsies, a visit to your local RV sales lot will leave you slack-jawed in astonishment. Instead of the old porta-potty facilities of yesteryear, you'll find complete baths, including sunken tubs, showers and designer vinyls. Microwaves and deep-freezers are all but standard, as are three-way refrigerators which operate on either propane, the rig's 12-volt battery system or 110-volt park current. Furnishings are lush and tastefully matched to the rest of the decor, and an ingenious use of space provides incredible storage room. Therefore, it isn't surprising that many folks spend a lot of time in their RVs during retirement when they finally have time to enjoy them to the fullest.

RV Parks Galore

RV destinations offer accommodations that vary in quality from super deluxe to extra grungy. Prices vary from costly to free. Later on, you'll find out how you can even get paid to park! Higher-quality parks generally have certain features in common besides higher prices: swimming pools, Jacuzzis and shuffleboard courts, sometimes even golf courses.

An all-important part of the better RV parks is a clubhouse. It's more than just a place to go for a cup of coffee and to meet other RV enthusiasts. The park clubhouse serves as the headquarters for the park's social activities. Dancing, bingo, arts and crafts, jazzercise, card parties, pot lucks and group tours are just a few of the organized pastimes available in the typical clubhouse. There's no excuse for ever being bored.

Space rentals in regular parks vary from as low as $50 a month to well over $300. For example, the most expensive park in Tucson, Arizona, charges $355 a month (plus electricity) for the winter months, but only $1,545 for year-round rent. That figures out to less than $130 a month. About half of the spaces are rented out for the year, with the owners leaving their rigs parked there during the summer. The park supplies a full-time social director for the season, with a complete calendar replete with tennis tournaments, swimming, hobbies and just about anything else one might wish to do. "Our people don't just sit around twiddling their thumbs," says the park manager. "We don't give them the chance to be bored."

From these costly heights, prices decrease, depending on the quality and location. Many perfectly adequate RV parks charge as little as $150 a month. One lady remarked, "Our park rent here costs us less than our oil bill if we stay home all winter, so I figure we're staying here for free. We just weatherproof our house and forget it until the snow melts!"

Not long ago I read an ad in *Trailer Life* for an RV park in Mesa, Arizona. It advertised low rates and an astonishing range of attractions. I'll list them here so you can see what you get for your money: clubhouse, ballroom, lounge, library, pool/billiards, card parlor, Olympic pool/Jacuzzi, kitchen/snack bar, four tennis courts, putting green, golf driving cage, shuffleboard and horseshoes, exercise gym, lapidary shop, silversmith studio, woodworking shop, ceramics studio, arts and crafts, ping pong, laundry/ironing rooms and sewing room. Apparently the only hobbies missing are bungee-cord jumping, goldfish-swallowing and underwater basket weaving.

Those addicted to slot machines will find many of Nevada's casinos very accommodating for RV travelers. For example, last time we looked, Sam's Town RV park in Las Vegas charged about $10 per night, which includes (besides hookups) a 56-lane bowling alley, 2,000 slot machines, two floors of casino with keno and a race-and-sports book. As if that isn't enough, they offer free dance lessons. Most casinos don't bother charging for parking; they simply request that RVs park in a designated area, but provide no hookups. By the way, some of Nevada's gambling casinos, starting with Harold's Club in Reno, have made it a policy to hire senior citizens as part-time or full-time workers. How would you feel about dealing a few hands of blackjack next winter?

The variety of RV parks almost defies description. Those with their own golf courses present a country-club atmosphere, complete with 19th-hole cocktail lounges and gourmet dining rooms. Others sit right on the beach for easy access to surf-casting and splashing around in your bathing suits.

There are even parks for nudists, where people splash around in their birthday suits! That's right, scattered about the U.S. and Canada are at least a hundred clothing-optional RV parks, where you can swim, play tennis or ride bikes in the buff, if you so choose. Ordinarily, you must be a member of American Sunbathing Association to enter, but most parks allow trial visits by respectable-looking couples. Monthly RV space rents are usually quite reasonable—$185 a month at one deluxe naturist park in Florida, including full use of facilities, electricity, water and garbage. Since park residents do laundry less frequently, they also save on laundry detergent.

What Will the Kids Think?

A big problem for many retirees who want to start full-timing in their RVs is the shock, disbelief and disapproval of their children. They cannot believe that their parents could do such a thing. The whole idea seems irresponsible to them. "Why do they want to worry us like this? Why do they have to do weird things? Why can't they stay home and be like everyone else?" Yet, they forget how we were appalled at the weird clothes they used to wear or by their behavior at those gawdawful rock concerts.

As one lady put it, "My only real problem getting started into full-timing was convincing my children, relatives and friends that I had not lost all my senses. To them, 'Grandmother' means dressing in a long skirt, apron, bonnet and high-top shoes. She is a person who sits by the fire, knitting sweaters while cookies bake in the oven. 'Grandmother' certainly doesn't mean flitting around the country alone in a little motorhome, dressed in a sweatshirt, jeans and sneakers!"

If you want to humor the kids a bit, you can put a CB radio or cellular phone into your rig and get car insurance with a good emergency road service provision. But in the final analysis, it's your retirement, and now it's your turn to worry them a little.

One caution that all experienced full-timers will give to newcomers: don't burn your bridges. You may want to recross them should you decide that full-timing is not as romantic as you thought. If you own a home, you might consider leasing it out for a year or two, "just to make sure." Some make arrangements with their tenants to reserve the garage, perhaps a room or the basement for storing their things. Renters can also forward mail and telephone messages.

We've talked to many retirees who started out as fulltimers, convinced that they would never again be "tied down" to a house, but who eventually found their dream home and settled down. One couple we interviewed sold everything and moved into their fifth-wheel, fully confident that this would be their life for the next decade. But a week later, they stumbled upon a town which they fell in love with. They ended up trading their rig for a mobile home and that was the end of their full-timing experience.

RV Clubs and Retirement

Many RV travelers feel that part of the fun of owning a rig comes from belonging to a club. Rallies, camp-outs and tours are just a few of the organized activities available through RV clubs. Newsletters keep members well informed about upcoming events. Depending upon the season and weather, club members meet at designated campgrounds, set up an enclave and start socializing. There are clubs for rockhounds and prospectors, for jewelry-making, quilting, handicapped travelers, computer buffs and just about any kind of hobby you can imagine and for which you aren't likely to be arrested. Anything you want to know about RV lifestyles, you will learn by belonging to one or more clubs.

For the full-time RV traveler, however, club membership is more than just an entertaining pastime; membership is essential. Folks who scrimp by on very limited budgets and who must squeeze the maximum value from every dollar do not hesitate spending money for club dues. They consider club membership every bit as important as gasoline when living full time in their rigs.

Club publications present news of rallies, of new campgrounds and keep you posted on other members' whereabouts. Some list free parking places provided by members for the overnight use of fellow members. The sticker on your RV announcing that you are a member breaks the ice with an invitation for other members to introduce themselves. You are able to enjoy the inexpensive benefits of RV ownership without feelings of uneasiness about being a stranger among strangers.

The largest RV club of all, Good Sam, started 25 years ago when a Utah trailerist sent a letter to *Trail-R-News* magazine (now *Trailer Life*). The letter suggested that the magazine offer subscribers a decal for their rigs, something that would indicate their willingness to stop and help fellow RVers in distress. The idea caught on and mushroomed into the Good Sam Club.

Since few insurance companies were interested in covering RVs, it seemed only natural that the club should provide policies tailored to members' needs. Before long it became the major insurer of travel trailers and motorhomes.

Today the Good Sam Club boasts over 750,000 members with 2200 chapters around the country. In addition to insurance with emergency road service, policy holders receive discounts at hundreds of campgrounds in the Good Sam Park program, a campground directory, a subscription to *Trailer Life* magazine, trip routing and even RV financing. (The insurance isn't mandatory for club membership.) Free services include mail forwarding, credit card loss protection, lost key service, lost pet service, commission-free travelers checks and a monthly news magazine, the *Hi-Way Herald*.

Trailer Life, by the way, is a valuable publication for RV travelers, whether full-timers or weekenders. It is full of important news, features on how to repair your rig and interesting places to visit as well as general trends in the RV industry. Information on Good Sam Club can be obtained from P.O. Box 11097, Des Moines, IA 50381; (800) 234-3450.

Several clubs specialize in serving the needs of those who live full time in their RVs. The best-known and largest is the Escapees (SKP) with 12,000 members. Founded by Joe and Kay Peterson several years ago, the club has grown by leaps and bounds as more and more people discover the joys of full-timing.

The Escapees' national headquarters is at 100 Rainbow Dr., Livingston, TX 77351; (800) 976-8377. The club publishes a monthly news magazine covering important news about rallies and get-togethers, new places to park, tips on equipment maintenance and hints for making life easier for people who make their homes on the road. Members report where they are and what they've been doing so friends can keep in touch. SKP members often remark, "We feel like we're part of a large, close-knit family."

Another important facility of the club is a mail forwarding and message service. An 800 number both accepts phone messages and allows you to retrieve them. Mail is forwarded automatically. This solves the problem of keeping in touch with the world while gypsying.

Unmarried RV travelers have their own clubs. A group known as Loners on Wheels is the one we know best. All the members we've interviewed are enthusiastic about the club and continually talk about what it has done for them.

As part of the research for this book, my wife and I decided to visit a Loners on Wheels gathering to see first-hand what it was all about. So, one balmy January evening we drove our motorhome off the pavement to make camp amongst thousands of trailers, campers and motorhomes in the California desert setting of Slab City.

It was a pleasant, moonlit night, with a slight breeze blowing in from the nearby Salton Sea. We breathed deeply of sagebrush-perfumed air as we walked across the sandy desert to where the Loners on Wheels had their semi-permanent headquarters. Several official trailers were set up around a large cement slab, which served as a dance floor at night and as a shuffleboard court by day.

We explained that we were interviewing retirees and were interested in talking to single retirees. We had come to the right place; the campers were eager to talk to us. "Man or woman—life is a difficult experience to handle alone," remarked one single man who had just moved into retirement. "I've found the solution to my loneliness through RV travel and belonging to Loners on Wheels."

As is the case at most Loners on Wheels camp-outs, about 60 percent of the campers here were women. I asked one lady, "How do you feel about safety out here in the desert?" She explained that she had been a bank teller before retirement, and added, "During the two years before I retired, I was held up at gunpoint five times! Now, ask me again how safe I feel here!"

Another woman, a widow, said, "If it weren't for this club and all of the wonderfully supportive friends in it, tonight I would be sitting alone watching television in a two-room apartment in downtown Seattle." She smiled at her friends and said, "I've never felt safer in my life."

"Traveling with friends makes all the difference in the world," explained another LoW member. "I'd never have the courage to do it alone." With other club members in a caravan—always ready and willing to assist—RV traveling becomes relatively anxiety-free. Socializing over breakfast, cooking dinner together or singing around the evening campfire, there is no time to be bored or feel alone. Since most RV clubs have a philosophy of "Never let a stranger into camp without a hug," RV retirement becomes a heart-warming experience.

Free Lodging in State and National Parks

Perhaps the main reason you wanted an RV in the first place was to visit scenic national parks, recreational wonderlands and picturesque parts of the country. Making camp alongside a lakeside glade or beside a sparkling trout stream—that's what it's all about, right? Most folks, restricted to a two-week vacation, have to squeeze in any campsite where they can make reservations. When park campsites are full, it's off to an $18-a-night commercial park with hundreds of grubby children screaming underfoot.

However, if you're retired and have your own transportable housing, you may make application as a campground volunteer. If you're accepted, the park will reserve a prime campsite for you at no cost whatsoever! You can stay the season for free. Even better, some parks will even pay you to park for the entire season! While the pay may be minimal, the work is also minimal, yet interesting and rewarding.

Every vacation season, county, state and national parks are in need of paid and volunteer workers. So are private resorts, campgrounds and tourist attractions. Often, housing units are there for the workers, but space is limited; living accommodations can be provided for only so many people, the rest must be turned away. However, when you bring your own housing with you, it's a different story. They love their RV staff members!

Since many volunteer and paid jobs are in rustic locations, managers and employers are delighted to find seasonal workers who need nothing more than water and electricity hookups. Then, when the season is over, the workers pack up and move on to better weather, leaving behind nothing but good memories. Often before they leave, arrangements are made for the coming season.

Jobs opportunities are available as campground managers, bookkeepers, off-season caretakers, maintenance and gate-keepers. The most common volunteer jobs offer free parking and hookups (but no salary) to campground "hosts," whose duties consist of answering the questions of new campers and making them feel at home. Other jobs require more responsibility and offer a salary.

One couple called the local county parks department and asked if there were to be any openings for campground hosts at a particularly lovely park where they wanted to stay. "No," came the reply, "We don't use campground hosts." The lady calling asked, "Why not? It won't cost you anything." The head of the department thought that over for a moment, and then decided to give it a try. The couple parked their motorhome by the lake, hooked up to free power and spent the summer simply talking to visitors and answering questions.

We interviewed another couple who spent the summer of 1991 at a county park on a scenic whitewater river, a favorite place for river rafting and trout fishing. This was their first time doing this. "We sent out ten applications," Brenda said, "and within the week we received two positive replies. We took this one because it paid a monthly stipend as well as the free hookups." Her husband said, "They even installed a telephone in our trailer, so we could be in contact with park headquarters."

When asked how much their summer on the river cost them, they did some mental calculations, and Joe said, "We were spending about $65 a week at the market. We know, because we only drove into town twice a week. Our only other expenses were laundry, telephone calls to our kids and dinner out once a week." Brenda added, "Video cassettes, too. We rented four or five a week. No television here." After doing some work with a hand calculator, they came up with an average of $293 a month. They didn't mention their pay, but it surely covered a portion of their expenses.

RV Budgets

The question of how much it costs to live full-time in an RV is a complicated one. All of us have different incomes and budgets within which we must live. as widely as do our budgets. Those with huge mortgages on a deluxe motorhome will naturally spend a lot of their income on payments. Some spend a lot of time driving from place to place, consuming gasoline or diesel fuel and staying in fancy resorts every night. Getting from one place to another isn't cheap since fuel consumption is higher than with normal driving. But the average RV full-timer moves only to change locations for the season, and ideally, the rig will be paid for. Renting park space by the month rather than by the night reduces costs drastically. The truly economical lifestyles include a considerable amount of boondocking and freebies.

We talked to a lady who makes her home in a 24-foot motorhome, and she told us: "Last winter, when I left my Michigan home base to go to the California desert, I found I could easily get by on $350 a month." She went on to add that during the winter before she started full-timing, her fuel oil, gas and electric bills at home totaled close to $300 for one month, so getting by on $350 was easy.

Not everybody can manage full-timing on $350 a month, of course. We all know individuals who spend more than that on cigarettes and booze. Well, how did our friend do it? She stayed at California's Slab City for zero rent, where the gentle desert climate all but eliminated the need for heat or air conditioning (Slab City has no utility hookups anyway). She used three five-gallon tanks of propane for cooking and an occasional touch of warmth when the temperature dropped below 60 degrees outdoors. A solar panel supplemented her 12-volt system for lights, radio and cassette player (TV reception is lousy in Slab City). Therefore, her total utility costs came to less than $25 for the full three-month sojourn—an average of $8 per month.

"Since I am single, my food costs are low," she said. "Neighbors at Slab City always share rides for shopping in Niland, so I drove the two miles to town just once a week. I needed to dump my holding tanks anyway. My total driving was a little over 50 miles for the entire stay. My gasoline bill was almost nothing."

In addition, she shared expenses with three other single ladies for a day trip to Mexico (about an hour's drive), plus one overnight expedition to challenge the slot machines and blackjack tables in Nevada (about four and a half hours away). "We shared a large room—at the senior citi·

zen rate of $33 with two double beds—and we took advantage of the 99-cent breakfast specials and the enormous buffets in the casino restaurants. That was the only month that I spent $350, and then only because I couldn't make the slot machines pay off."

Seasonal Retirement

Trailers, campers and motorhomes by the hundreds of thousands flock toward winter retirement destinations in Texas, Florida, California and Arizona every winter. This is an ideal compromise for those who refuse to give up their paid-for homes or who cannot stand the thought of leaving their grandchildren permanently. For winter's duration, they golf, bicycle, stroll the beaches—whatever suits their fancy—instead of huddling inside next to the fireplace. If they feel like fishing, they needn't chop a hole in the ice first. Money saved on heating bills back home pays for a large part of the trip.

Other retirees, particularly those with homes near housing-hungry colleges or universities, make arrangements with faculty or students to rent their places while they travel. Apartment dwellers give notice in time for their November departure, and make application for another apartment for their return in March.

By nature, RV travelers are friendly folks. They have to be to enjoy parking shoulder-to-shoulder with their neighbors. You'll find few strangers in RV parks. Winter travelers generally have two sets of friends: those who live in their home town and those who live in the RV winter neighborhood. As winter parks begin receiving visitors, old friends meet and celebrate a joyous renewal of last year's companionship. "We've been coming here for the last six years," one lady told us, "and we have more friends in this park than we've ever made back home!"

The advantage of RV retirement is that you can be very selective about climate and/or geographical location. When you become bored with the scenery or with your neighbors, or when the fishing gets slow, you simply start your engine and roll on to greener pastures. Or, perhaps, to better fishing.

All part-timers don't travel seasonally; some use their rigs to visit friends and relatives scattered around the country. Since weather isn't the most important consideration, they travel during the uncrowded and inexpensive times of the year. One couple we interviewed has two sons living on the West Coast, a son in New Jersey and a daughter in Miami. "We make it a point to spend a month each year visiting," explained June, a petite brunette who helps drive the 30-foot motor home. "We never wear out our welcome, and we have our own home. We don't have to interfere with our children's privacy by staying in their homes."

Desert Boondocking

The southwestern desert areas draw hundreds of thousands of RVs, the vast majority driven by retired people, as they visit the cities and desert outback for winter stays. Snowbirds have become a major economic boon for host communities. Yuma, Arizona, for example, doubles its 50,000 population every winter. Phoenix hosts around 200,000 seasonal residents, bringing almost $200 million to the economy. A large number of these visitors bring RVs with them.

The Southwest offers plenty of conventional RV resorts with the usual recreation facilities. But for many, the desert Southwest presents unique opportunities for "boondocking," an ingenious technique of camping without paying overnight fees. "Freebies" is another expression for the same thing.

Most every RV owner boondocks occasionally; that's one of their rig's advantages. Roadside rest areas are perfect for getting sleepy RV drivers off the interstates. A supermarket parking lot can be a lifesaver when it's too late to find an RV park. A friend or relative's driveway is much better for a weekend visit than a motel or trailer park a dozen miles away.

Southwestern desert boondockers have raised the concept of boondocking to a fine art. A boondocker's badge of pride is their ability to spend the entire winter boondocking—enjoying sunshine, companionship and recreation—without spending a nickel for rent. Needless to say, free rent and no utilities help enormously toward the notion of shoestring retirement. It eliminates the two most expensive items in most budgets.

Desert boondocking started informally many years ago, when a few campers and trailers began pulling off the road onto government land and spending a few days or weeks just loafing. They'd simply set up camp wherever they pleased and make themselves at home midst the cactus and sagebrush. Because the vast majority of Arizona and California desert lands are public property, nobody complained. Before long, the word got out that free camping in the desert was the way to spend the winter. Every winter, small cities of campers began blossoming all over the desert.

Rather than attempt to evict thousands of RVs, the U.S. Bureau of Land Management (BLM) began selling camping permits for the entire season and encouraging the boondockers to congregate in certain locations. The fee is a mere $25 a year, which goes toward providing drinking water, dumping stations and clean-up. (This fee is due for a small increase and may be higher by the time of publication.) Recently, the BLM started offering free campsites (presumably with utilities) for volunteers who will do a small amount of work, monitoring the permit-holding campers and checking sanitary conditions.

Don't get the wrong impression and equate boondocking with poverty. You'll see some rigs boondocked in the desert that cost more than many fancy homes. Their owners can afford to spend the winter anywhere they care to, yet here they are, happy campers in the cactus. They come from all walks of life, all trades, professions and occupations.

Almost all desert boondockers are retired and have one thing in common: a love for outdoor winter retirement. To be sure, some really can't afford a winter vacation any other way. In fact some have to live this way because their incomes are so low. Therefore, you'll find shabby old homemade trailers and rustic campers on old pickups parked next to shiny new motorhomes and spiffy fifth-wheel trailers. RV camping is truly a social leveler. This is democracy at the grass-roots level (or is it cactus-roots level?).

In addition to the low rent of $25 for the season, boon-dockers enjoy the lowest utility bills imaginable. They pay nothing, since there are no 110-current plugs in the desert, no water hookups, no natural gas and no garbage/sewer charges. Bottled gas cooks meals and sometimes provides lights. Radios, TV and indoor lights are powered by 12-volt batteries, which are charged by solar panels. Conserving drinking water and battery power becomes second nature after a while. This is living at its simplest—and at its cheapest!

Those who prefer solitude simply wheel off the road wherever they choose—within the permit area, of course—and drive until all traces of civilization are out of sight. They set up camp and sometimes stay for weeks before having to make a run into the nearest town for supplies. They are disturbed by no sounds other than the distant yapping of coyotes or feisty little birds chattering away in the sagebrush. My understanding is that the BLM maintains ten campgrounds in Arizona and eight in eastern California, near the Colorado River. Some have improvements such as water and dumping stations, others very little. One, near Holtsville, California, is even said to have a hot tub!

Arizona Choices

Most folks can't stand solitude for very long. Now, you might imagine that desert RV camping would be isolation personified. Oddly enough, desert camping can be perfect for the gregarious, the talkative and those who love to make friends, as well as for hermits. This is because every winter, the biggest RV boondocking area of all—Quartzite, Arizona—changes from empty desert into a virtual city. Although rigs don't park cheek-to-jowl, as they must in commercial RV parks, the campers have to get close together to make room for the others. Because so many friendly neighbors are camped nearby, folks who normally wouldn't dream of boondocking feel absolutely secure here.

Some claim a million people converge upon Quartzite every winter. That's entirely possible, because when you drive toward Quartzite's center, RVs fill the desert as far as the eye can see. Other estimates (probably more accurate), peg the yearly roundup at 200,000. No one knows for sure, since rigs are continually arriving and departing or moving from one boondocking site to another. Whatever the population—200,000 or more—Quartzite becomes quite a city.

Throughout late spring, summer and early fall, Quartzite lives the life of a typical desert crossroads community. But when winter rolls around, things change quickly. Entrepreneurs of all descriptions set up shop, selling wares and services to the flood of RV owners who begin arriving in mid-fall. Hobbies become businesses and pre-retirement skills once again become valuable.

Signs on the front of motorhomes, campers and trailers announce: "Alterations and Tailoring," "Air Conditioners Serviced," "Ceramics," "Auto Repair," and "Rental Library." One motorhome advertised a copy machine and word processing (presumably the rig had its own generator). People set up stands in front of their rigs to sell knicknacks, clothing, arts and crafts, trinkets and essentials. Automobile mechanics carry tools in their pickups and bring the garage to your vehicle while they make repairs. One man, who deals in flea-market kinds of merchandise, said, "Whenever my wife and I spend the winter here, we always take home more money than we left with."

During the winter the crossroads is embraced by a carnival mood. Making friends, going to potlucks, dances and club meetings keep the social types busy, and trading paperbacks, conversations over campfires and card games are for the quieter types. An outdoor ballroom called the

"Stardusty" hosts twice-a-week dances. Then, when the late spring sun begins beating down on aluminum roofs, when air conditioning begins to sound nice, the rigs abandon their makeshift city to the baking heat of the desert summer.

As popular as Quartzite may be, no description of Arizona boondocking would be complete without mentioning Sidewinder and Algodones. Near Yuma, just off Interstate 8, is Sidewinder RV Park, and a few miles further is Sleepy Hollow, just across the Mexican border from the village of Algodones. Last I heard, monthly rates were reasonable, in the neighborhood of $100. Sleepy Hollow park features a band that plays for dances every weekend. The musicians are regulars who come here every winter.

Because it's an easy walk to the border, many RV residents cross over into Mexico to patronize inexpensive dentists in Algodones. Dental work such as bridges, caps and dentures—excellently crafted—cost a fraction of what you'd pay on this side of the border. Eyeglasses, frames and contact lenses are well-crafted, using the identical materials as in the states, but at drastic reductions in price. Medical treatments for everything from cancer to arthritis attract visitors from all over the country who are searching for cures to "incurable" problems. Laetril, and who knows what other medicines, are readily available there, treatments that are illegal on this side of the line.

Another encampment is located north of Yuma, around Imperial Lake and Dam. Campgrounds bear names such as "Hurricane Ridge" and "Beehive." Government-constructed restrooms, holding-tank dumps and fresh water make winter-long camping comfortable and inexpensive. (Free, if I'm not mistaken.)

California's Unique Slab City

During World War II, General Patton searched for a desert training ground to prepare his armored division for war. He wanted terrain that simulated North Africa's desert, a place to get his tank crews in shape for the planned invasion. He found it near the small town of Niland, not far from Southern California's Salton Sea. A large camp went up, the troops readied for battle. After the war, the camp was dismantled and abandoned, buildings razed to the ground, but the cement slabs upon which the buildings rested are still there—hence the name "The Slabs," or "Slab City."

These cement platforms made wonderful RV pads, so it wasn't long before a few campers began spending winters in the sunshine of the Southern California desert. The altitude is low, very close to sea level, making for winters which are as pleasant and balmy as the summers are hot and insufferable. The news quickly made the rounds of RV boondockers. Slab City became a rival to Quartzite. And, instead of the nominal $25 a year, Slab City is free!

Between 5,000 and 10,000 people congregate here every winter; by June, all but a handful are gone. RVs of all descriptions and prices pull off the paved road, head into the desert and park haphazardly, sometimes next to friends, other times seeking solitude. Compatible RVers cluster together, forming regular neighborhoods, each with a central campfire area surrounded by lawn chairs and chaise lounges.

The more religious campers have started a church, complete with regular services. The church, in a mobile home, doubles as an information center when services aren't underway. This must be how it was back in the covered wagon days, for amongst all of this chaos there is an admirable sense of community and order. There is a heartwarming, natural sense of respect for neighbors' rights.

With no formal rules or regulations, the residents seem to know instinctively just what to do as individuals to make things work. Even though there are no law enforcement officers, there are no lawbreakers. When an occasional troublemaker drifts into Slab City, he or she receives a silent treatment that is followed by determined group action should the offender not catch the hint.

An unspoken notion of the Golden Rule inspires folks to care for their neighbors. Should a camper not appear out-

side by 10 o'clock in the morning neighbors will check to
see if everything is okay. Several RV units have CB radios,
always monitoring channel nine, ready to call Niland
(about two miles away) for medical emergencies, or the
rare occasion when someone needs an ambulance or a sher-
iff's deputy. At any given time, a retired nurse or two will
be staying here, so medical care isn't as far away as it might
seem.

Although the majority of the Slabs' residents are retired,
a few younger families join the community every year. As
a matter of fact, a county school bus makes a daily stop to
pick up the handful of children who live there.

Once a month, a government agency out of San Diego
arrives with surplus commodities, and for some unknown
but generally appreciated reason, the Salvation Army
drops in two or three times a month to distribute vegeta-
bles, canned goods and other foods. Some campers need
this help; most don't, even though they welcome the freebies. As one lady said, "When you're living on Social
Security, you feel that anything the government hands out
is something your taxes have already paid for!"

With no rent or utilities, there is little to spend your
money on at the Slabs. Several retirees tell us that they not
only get by on their Social Security checks—they save some
of it every month! The Niland post office receives many a
retirement check for Slab City residents. The extra money
spent in the town doesn't go unnoticed by the town residents who deeply appreciate their winter neighbors. The
campers pump $4,000,000 yearly into the economy of
Imperial county.

Not everyone will be happy at Slab City, though. My
wife and I agree that it's fun for a while and that we thoroughly enjoy the extremely interesting mixture of campers.
Yet a long-term visit here could grow tiresome. It's a long
journey to the nearest decent library, bookstore or shopping center. Before long, we catch up on our reading, grow
tired of playing cards with neighbors and grow weary of
eating our own cooking and begin dreaming of Chinese
food and pizza with sausage and anchovies. For a while, I

enjoy not worrying about deadlines or telephones, but the truth is, after a while, I miss them.

Texas' Rio Grande Valley

Another important destination for RV retirees is in the great state of Texas. RV parks throughout Texas draw travelers from all over the United States and Canada. Although Texas undoubtedly has boondocking locations, the emphasis here is on traditional RV parks. The main attraction is that part of Texas bordering Mexico: the Rio Grande Valley, a country famous for truck farms, grapefruit groves, and nowadays, groves of RV parks.

Each winter, trailers, campers and motorhomes of all descriptions converge on the Rio Grande valley and become seasonal abodes for several hundred thousand temporary retirees. "Winter Texans," they're called. They are welcomed by the local businessmen and residents who acknowledge the tremendous boost retirees give the economy. Orange groves, palm trees and 80-degree afternoons make for pleasant living while winter winds paralyze the countryside back home.

Winter retirement in south Texas isn't a particularly new idea. It started back in the 1930s, when Midwestern farmers, their activities shut down by cold weather, would make their way to the warmth and sunshine of the Rio Grande Valley. Pulling old-style house trailers or driving homemade campers, these cold-weather refugees began arriving in such numbers that the Rio Grande Valley area gained the nickname of "the poor man's Florida." When RVs came into their own, and lost the connotation of "poor," the Rio Grande Valley came into its own as a retirement eden.

The number of winter visitors keeps growing. Ten years ago, about 50,000 snowbirds wintered in the Brownsville-Harlingen-McAllen area; today they number more than 200,000! A boom in RV park construction is trying to accommodate the crush. There are well over 500 parks around here, some with several hundred spaces each. One popular RV retirement destination is Mission, near McAllen. More than 10,000 RVs arrive here every winter, with 100 RV parks making room for them. They almost double the year-round population of Mission, which bills itself as "The Mecca for Winter Texans."

An interesting contrast exists between the lifestyles of the Desert Boondockers and the Winter Texans. While the desert folks pride themselves on living frugally, organizing unique social groups and creating their own entertainment, the Texas crowd prefers having things done for them. Since RV parks are big business here, they compete for winter residents by offering complete programs of entertainment and activities.

Social directors plan pancake breakfasts, ice cream socials, square dances and other events to get people mingling and having a good time. Swimming pools, hobby rooms and classes are common features as well as indoor shuffleboard, tennis, dance halls, libraries, pool rooms, sewing rooms and other special halls for recreation and socializing. Even bare-bones parks usually have a lively rec hall to go with laundry facilities. Park rents here are over $300 a month for the truly ritzy places and down to $200 for the more ordinary—certainly within the range of shoe-string retirement.

With such a tremendous influx of people every season, pressure is put on stores, restaurants and service enterprises to keep up with the additional demand for goods and services. This naturally creates a demand for seasonal workers. Many retirees state that they have no problem finding work if they so desire. Many RV parks hire their extra help exclusively from their seasonal residents. Some RVers have "steady" jobs, in that they work for the same employer every year.

McAllen is the largest town in this network of retirement cities with Mission, Harlingen and Brownsville filling out the list. Near the mouth of the Rio Grande is South Padre Island, a long, narrow spit of land that also draws RVs. The southernmost tip is covered by the town of South

Padre, but just a few miles north civilization gives way to sand dunes, good fishing and RV boondocking.

We've only discussed a small portion of RV seasonal retirement here. Excellent winter RV parking can be found throughout the southern parts of the United States, from Florida to the West Coast. For summer travel the selection is even wider in the north and into Canada.

Wintering in Mexico

Since Texas and the desert Southwest wintering places are so close to the Mexican border, it would be surprising if RV owners didn't venture further south for sun and tourism. Of course they do, and they've discovered some uniquely economical places to spend the winter. You will see RVs and RV caravans in all parts of the republic from the U.S. border to Guatemala. Hundreds of RV parks accommodate trailers, campers and motorhomes of all descriptions. For more details about the RV touring in Mexico, see my book RV Travel In Mexico.

The most popular RV winter retirement areas are found in the Baja California Peninsula and in the mainland state of Sonora. Baja is particularly well liked, partly because the peninsula is so dry that much of it is all but uninhabitable and boondocking is "in." Many wonderful beaches have no hotels or tourist accommodations; they spread empty and desolate along the beautiful Sea of Cortez or the rolling Pacific. Without an RV, no matter how rich you might be, you can only glimpse these sights as you drive past. With your own rolling home, you can enjoy beaches and scenery that those poor millionaires must forego.

Almost totally unimproved, these beaches are ideal for self-contained RVs that need no electricity, water or sewer system. A trip to the nearest town every week or two to replenish the drinking water supply does just fine. Like Slab City and Quartzite, the word about freebies and boondocking leaked out and thousands of RVs started making the winter trek to Baja's sunny winter clime. Like birds flocking together, they cluster along the shores and congregate wherever fishing and scenic attractions beckon.

Not unexpectedly, as more and more "Winter Mexicans" crowd the beaches, natives are see commercial possibilities, and they naturally want their share. Beaches often belong to "ejidos," or Indian communal lands, under tribal control. Even though all Mexican beaches are open to the public, ejidos can charge for overnight parking. That's why many beaches today are no longer free—although they might as well be because camping charges are so low.

Typically, a caretaker makes the rounds every evening and asks for a couple of dollars or so to park overnight— depending on the beach. In return, the caretakers make sure things are tidy and keep their eye out for suspicious characters.

The beach where we've spent the most time is Santispac, just south of Mulegé, about halfway down the peninsula. Several hundred RVs arrive here every winter, starting in October and staying until the weather begins heating up in April. With their rigs lined up along the beach, campfire pits in front, and sometimes a palm thatch "palapa" built for shade, these Americans and Canadians enjoy a bountiful season of companionship, fishing, swimming and just plain loafing.

Beach caretakers also keep their eyes on trailers and palapas left throughout the summer when Baja sunshine makes Death Valley seem cool. From the reports we get, theft is rarely a problem.

"The same folks tend to come to our special beach every season," explains one lady. "It's like a big homecoming every time another rig pulls in. With campfires every evening, it's like a three-month beach party." Her husband adds, "With rent almost free, it costs us less than $300 a month to spend the winter in Mexico. It could be less, but we like to eat breakfast at the beach restaurant and we often eat dinner in town."

For those who hesitate to boondock (although with a hundred rigs in a row, it hardly seems like boondocking), over a hundred RV parks are scattered about Baja. You'll find one just about anywhere you'd care to visit, as well as places you wouldn't visit on a bet. Facilities range from super-luxurious, five-star resorts to rustic fishing camps with no amenities other than hospitality, cold beer and friendly faces. (What else do you need?)

By the way, 99 percent of your RV neighbors will be from the United States or Canada, because Mexicans almost never own RVs. The ones who can afford them prefer to stay in first-class hotels when traveling. They don't understand why we think traveling in a small tin box is fun. (I don't either, but it is fun.)

Space rents for RV parks range from a couple dollars a day to one luxury place that charges as much as $35 a day. One of our favorite commercial parks is at Bahía de Los Angeles. There, a cement patio and an electrical hookup cost about $6 a day. A water truck passes through with drinking water and will fill your tanks for about $1.50.

The sea provides a bountiful harvest of clams and scallops, not to mention fish for those willing to toss a line in the water. Kids knock on the door every evening to see if you want to buy their freshly-caught fish or live pin scallops, still in the shell. A nearby restaurant serves excellent meals of fish, lobster and tough but tasty Mexican steaks.

Two little markets in the village supply rudimentary foods such as chickens, coffee, and sterilized milk. Folks on tight budgets are able to depend on the sea for much of their food, with clam chowder, sauteed scallops or rockfish fillets "Veracruzano" providing wonderful gourmet dinners.

"We load up our cabinets with canned goods and such before we leave San Diego," said one lady in Bahía de Los Angeles. "We seldom have to buy groceries here other than fresh eggs and tortillas from the "tienda" and veggies from local gardens. We feel as if we are eating for free. We made a deal for two month's space rent at $190, so I don't see how we could possibly spend more than $500 out of pocket for two months," said her husband, "and that's including the gas to get here and back!"

When driving in Baja during our last trip, I counted the number of vehicles on the road and noted that about half of them were RVs with U.S. or Canadian license plates. Sometimes it looked as if we "norteamericanos" had taken over the peninsula for our own campgrounds.

My personal experience has been very positive in Mexico after many years of driving cars, jeeps, motorhomes and pulling a vacation trailer. We've handed out questionnaires to RV travelers in Mexico, and one of the questions concerned safety. Unanimously, people said they felt very secure driving in Mexico. That shouldn't be too surprising, because otherwise they wouldn't be there.

North for a Cool Summer

Seasonal travel is not the snowbirds' exclusive kingdom. Summer heat and humidity send thousands on the reverse trek. Retirees who select Phoenix or Tucson for retirement because of their lovely winter weather can be bored silly by endless, 100-degree-plus July and August days. That's why you'll see Arizona license plates in Montana, Michigan and Maine during the summer. Spring and fall may be beautiful in Missouri and Indiana, but summers are suffocating and could better be spent elsewhere.

We interviewed one Phoenix couple who regularly visits the Oregon coast each summer. Their favorite town, Brookings, seldom sees summer highs above 70 degrees, and the couple always sleeps under an electric blanket. "We've never used the motorhome's air conditioner in Brookings," the husband said, adding, "We've never seen the temperature reach 80 degrees!" Other RVs visit here in the winter as well, since fishing is good all year, and it never freezes. Be prepared for rain, however.

Folks who choose to retire on the Gulf coast of Florida because of mild winters dearly love to escape the hot summers there. The hills of West Virginia, North Carolina, Kentucky and Tennessee offer welcome deliverance from Florida's steamy summers. The Atlantic coast, particularly up around Maine, offers some delightfully cool places to park and relax. This might be the time to visit those Canadian RV friends you see every year in your winter neighborhood.

Although RVs are fine for escaping winter cold or summer heat, they are seldom practical for bitterly cold weather. Northern states like North Dakota, Idaho or Vermont—any place where below-zero temperatures are the winter rule rather than exception—are too frigid for all but a few RVs; they're mostly designed for sunny climes. Scanty insulation in the walls and nothing beneath the floors will invalidate all your propane heater's most heroic efforts. Furthermore, RV plumbing is flimsy at best and freezes solid at the first hint of a cold snap.

Of course, a few of the more expensive units are especially designed for full-time living, including winters. They are better-insulated; some are even heated with fuel oil furnaces, rather than inefficient propane or catalyst heaters. They also have electrically heated water pipes to keep them from bursting. But you'll have to love cold weather to enjoy RVs in sub-freezing weather.

Chapter Eleven

Singles and Retirement

Perhaps you've noticed that the ads in most retirement publications picture typical retirees as a handsome couple, tenderly holding hands as they gaze lovingly upon their new retirement home (or Cadillac or yacht, whatever the ad is selling). The husband is attired in an Irish-tweed sportcoat, and his distinguished platinum-toned hair sweeps back from an aristocratic forehead. (He's never bald as a pig's knuckle, now is he?) The wife's hairdo discretely displays a few silver highlights; if we didn't know she was retired we'd assume she was about 37 years old. This typical retired couple is successful, affluent and looking forward to a future of golf games, gourmet dinners and bridge parties as they entertain brilliantly in their fabulous new home.

You don't need someone to tell you that this picture is far from accurate. Besides the fact that few of us men can brag about our aristocratic-looking foreheads, most of us actually look our ages and some are truly bald as pigs' knuckles. More importantly, a large percentage of retirement-aged people lack that loving other person to hold hands with. A huge number approach retirement alone. Furthermore, they find themselves far from affluent, with their minds on other matters than bridge and golf games.

What happens when your spouse dies unexpectedly, just before your planned retirement date? All your plans get knocked into that famous cocked hat. What about the homemaker who spent her productive years raising a family, only to find herself divorced once the children are on their own. Where do you go from here?

Women and Retirement

For every 100 older men in the United States, there are 146 older women. This ratio increases with age to a high of 260 women for each 100 men for those 85 and older. Only 41 percent of these women are married, compared to 78 percent of the men. Furthermore, more than half of America's women are on their own even before they reach retirement age—by the time they are 55 years old.

Those divorced or widowed women who manage to find careers in the workplace often find their social lives revolving around work. But once single women leave the workplace, they find a void that needs to be filled by friends and family. Should a retired woman be short on either of these commodities, she faces a lonely future. Chances are, she will also be short on retirement funds. It's well known that women earn significantly less than men for equal work, so they end up with lower Social Security payments, company pensions and savings accounts.

Women also have fewer options or activities that society considers "acceptable" and with which they feel comfortable. A man can be perfectly happy tent camping and fishing in the woods, wearing the same socks a week at a time. Most retired single women not only feel uncomfortable camping in a flimsy tent, but hate fishing in the first place. (Not to mention dirty socks.) A man thinks nothing of living just about anywhere, but most women feel apprehensive in all but the most secure situations.

It's no secret that women earn far less than men, even when performing the same work. Also, their working careers are shorter, many of them taking time out from the job to care for children, returning to the workplace only after a divorce or death of the spouse. A single woman's financial base is typically very low.

Furthermore, because of age discrimination, women are often pressured to quit work and draw their Social Security at age 62 rather than wait until maximum benefits are due. Finding part-time work is also more difficult for a woman. The result of women's lifetime of low incomes are Social Security checks which are about half that of a man's who earned good wages all his working life. Single people, both men and women, need different retirement strategies than married couples to survive on a shoestring. But single women need miracles.

Single Transitions

One might assume that transition into retirement would be easy for those who never married, or for those who have lived much of their adult lives as single persons. Why should retirement be a traumatic experience? After all, aren't they used to a single life? It might seem that the only thing to do now is adjust to a lifestyle that doesn't include working every day. Yet these people often find retirement especially lonely, particularly if their entire social life had centered around their jobs. At work, they had fellow employees to socialize with, friends to talk with and companions at lunch. When they stop working, suddenly all of that is gone. Also gone are regular paychecks, paid health care benefits and Christmas bonuses. It's a different world out there when you quit work.

For those fortunate enough to have built up a network of friends and acquaintances, leaving this umbrella probably doesn't make much sense. Even though you're living in an expensive area, you might be better off squeezing by and keeping your friends and your mode of living.

But if your friends do come mostly from your business or workplace world, and if you have few or no nearby family connections, you could find that you have little to lose by going someplace more economical, perhaps someplace with a nicer climate. You can then start building a new life, acquiring new friends and exploring new interests. If you're already living in a high-cost area, moving to someplace more economical might be the ticket to a better life.

In many economical retirement locations, particularly in small towns, small furnished apartments can be found for less than $300 a month, including utilities. These apartments are small, but perfectly adequate for a single person trying to get by on a shoestring. Not long ago, we looked at a small studio apartment in a small town on Oregon's Rogue River—a delightfully peaceful and pretty place for economical living. The rent was about $275. Shopping was a four-minute walk from the door. A single woman would feel perfectly safe here.

Once settled, you can see how you like the area, try making friends and exploring a new lifestyle. As a new kid on the block, you'll find the best way to begin accumulating a new set of friends and acquaintances is through volunteer work. Go to the local senior citizens' office and apply for work with RSVP or whatever volunteer program that's available. Within days, you'll start building a new network, and before long you will have more friends than you ever made through working every day. One of our correspondents, a retired man, told us that his strategy for making friends is through square-dancing. He says, "Just check with the clubs (Elks, Eagles, American Legion, etc.) as well as with the chamber of commerce."

Shared Housing

Earlier we discussed the concept of shared housing, a particularly effective way for singles to find inexpensive living quarters. Renting a room in a house requires little commitment—while you investigate a new locality for retirement potential. The bonus is that you are not alone; housemates act as a surrogate family. House sharing is a particularly successful strategy for older women, when two, three or four pool their resources and enjoy a dignified, comfortable living arrangement. House sharing by singles is also a creative technique for living in an exclusive, high-rent area on a limited income. Remember, as an added bonus, the crime rates in expensive areas are generally low.

It can be very lonely cooking for one person in an empty house. A person who owns a home often finds that a compatible companion or two sharing house expenses makes perfectly good sense. (On the other hand, it could make equally good sense to sell the house, put the money into stocks and move in with someone else.)

House or apartment sharing opportunities are becoming more and more common by the day. A glance at any newspaper classified section usually turns up several ads seeking this kind of arrangement. Screen the candidates carefully to make sure you like and trust them. It goes without saying that compatibility is the highest-ranking consideration in house sharing.

Retirement Communities

Not everyone can be comfortable pulling up stakes and relocating as a stranger in a strange town or living in someone else's home. A convenient, worry-free alternative for singles is the concept of a non-prepay retirement community, the kind where you simply rent by the month. Again, I'll use an Oregon example. We looked at a retirement community in a mid-sized city in the central part of the state. At that point a studio apartment was renting for less than $700 a month. This included three meals daily (served in the dining room), weekly housekeeping and linen service, 24-hour staffing, cable TV, social and recreational programs, scheduled transportation, off-street parking and all utilities except telephone. Thus, aside from medical insurance, clothing and phone use, your basic expenses are covered for around $700 a month! For many singles, Social Security covers it. Of course, this facility is not exclusively for singles; for an additional $275 monthly, a couple receives the same services. A similar place in the same town charged $880 for slightly better accommodations, but this still seems like a shoestring to me.

Several advantages accrue to this type of living arrangement. Besides the fact that your living costs are absolutely predictable, you can explore the community to see whether this is desirable for your long-term retirement without having to make any serious commitment. The manager of this retirement facility points out that she encourages people to do a three-month trial before pulling up stakes in their home towns or doing anything drastic. "This is particularly important upon the death of a spouse. Too often the survivor isn't capable of making rational decisions for the time being. They feel isolated, lonely, with no stimulation, and trapped in an empty home. In a retirement community they are surrounded by friendly people; they take their meals in the dining room surrounded by other residents with whom to communicate. Since you have no long-term obligations, this is a relatively painless way to try out a new lifestyle as well as trying on a new community for size."

One caution: most residents will be older; there are no multi-generational retirement homes. Some residents will be quite old—this is their last step before entering a rest home. So, you might look around and see if you'll find compatible companions, retirees your own age and enthusiasm to relate with. Just because you're retired doesn't mean you're old!

Don't think the above-mentioned retirement community is unique. You'll find similar establishments all over the country. To locate them, simply open up the Yellow Pages to "Retirement," and some will surely be listed. To choose a retirement community in another city, visit your local library and ask for the section where they keep out-of-town phone books. Then choose the city or town where you might want to retire, check the listings for something that sounds nice, and do some shopping for price and quality. Don't expect to find a $700 or $800 monthly fee just anywhere. Charges vary widely, depending upon the community, the area's cost of living and the quality of the facility.

Be careful about those places where you must "buy-in" to the facility or where you must sign a long-term lease. There is nothing wrong with these concepts; it's just that if you are looking around for low-cost retirement alternatives you probably aren't interested in putting up $50,000 nonrefundable front money just to see whether you like your new retirement location. If you find you aren't happy, you would be in a far better position if all you were responsible for was a 30-day notice before you shove off. Also, don't expect to find these reasonable rents in a larger city or in an expensive area. Like everything else in an expensive location, the costs are likely to be extravagant, too.

When you find something you can afford, check it out. The best time to visit is for lunch or dinner, when you can sample the quality and variety of the food. How is the place decorated? How does the staff interact with residents? Are they professional, yet caring? Is the place quiet or noisy? Do people seem friendly and do they socialize well? Don't hesitate to speak with residents and see how they like living there. Many retirement communities have furnished guest apartments set up for trial visits. At the least, arrange to stay a weekend to get the feel of the place.

Travel Clubs for Singles

During the research on this book, I came across a very interesting singles club, oriented around travel and putting singles in touch with each other. The national leader in the travel partner matching field is Travel Companion Exchange (TCE), of Amityville, New York. TCE brings together travelers of similar interests through a newsletter and computer match-up service. Members list their interests and describe the kind of travel companion they would like to find.

Traveling with a companion brings down costs considerably, because single travelers pay a high penalty for traveling alone. A room for one person often costs exactly the same as for two people. Therefore, it makes good sense to team up with someone to share experiences and expenses.

"This isn't a lonely hearts club or a dating service," says Jens Jurgen, the company president, "although it works well in that respect. We've had a lot of marriages. I remember one elderly lady who met and married a gentleman through the service. Then, a few years later I saw her name on the list again. Her husband died on a trip on the Orient Express, so she signed up to find another one!"

While men travelers more often prefer to travel with women, women more often prefer other women as companions—it's much less complicated that way. Sometimes a woman will seek a male companion on a strictly hands-off basis; they simply tour and dine together. Jurgen says, "I realize that opposite sex matches are not always platonic, but this does not trouble me. I'm catering to the needs of single people needing traveling companions."

For inexperienced, elderly or handicapped travelers, having a partner makes sense. Women traveling alone miss out a lot by being reluctant to visit some very interesting places. It goes without saying that you must be very careful when using this kind of service. You need to make it quite clear as to what the traveling relationship will be and what it will not be. TCE suggests that you meet and do some getting to know one another before setting out on adventures. One woman complained that her lady traveling companion "smoked like a chimney and wouldn't drive under 80 miles an hour." A few meetings beforehand might have avoided subsequent bad feelings. Though TCE is multi-generational in nature, there are plenty of retired members. Contact: Travel Companion Exchange, Box 833, Amityville, NY 11701.

Chapter Twelve

Foreign Retirement

Not as easy as it once was, it's still entirely possible to retire in a foreign country on a shoestring budget. But not in just any foreign country. The sad fact of life is that the U.S. dollar has been on a downslide for the past 15 years. And the Canadian dollar has been going down with it.

Gone are the days of the "Europe on $25 a Day" guidebooks. At one time, anyone with dollars in their jeans felt like a millionaire, sipping wine in Paris cafés, savoring Beef Wellington in a London restaurant or playing roulette in Monaco. A 15th-century stone cottage with a view of the Mediterranean rented for $100 a month, and a sumptuous meal—including wine—cost $2. Many retired North Americans routinely traveled abroad to spend several months a year in Province or on the Costa del Sol, because it was cheaper than staying home. No longer. Today you'll feel like an indigent in most of Europe. Even the cheapest places are as costly as here. And, it costs a fortune to get there. The Europe on a shoestring travel days are over.

Despite the low state of the dollar, a few foreign countries still exist where a shoestring budget can sustain a dignified and exciting lifestyle. Not in Europe, but much closer to home: in Mexico and Central America. Since the places I endorse don't require nearly the investment to visit (you can travel by bus if you like), long stays are far less expensive.

However, I feel extremely uneasy recommending foreign retirement to anyone who has little cash in reserve and whose income can be measured with a shoestring. Too many unknown and unexpected expenses inevitably crop up when living in a foreign country. Another problem: on a minimal income, you probably won't qualify for year-round residency, so you'll have to make periodic trips out of the country for specified durations before you can return. These trips can quickly run your living costs up.

Yes, you can live on a shoestring budget in some countries, but if you have to live on a shoestring budget, don't even think about it. At least at home, a series of "safety nets" of sorts will catch you should sudden disaster strike. City, county and state agencies will usually make sure you are somehow taken care of in emergency situations. Few countries give welfare assistance to foreigners. When trouble strikes, you are on your own or dependent upon the good graces of fellow North Americans. Furthermore, if you are truly indigent, most governments take a very dim view of your being there. Rarely are you permitted to work, and you'll get into trouble should you try.

But, if you have healthy backup funds, you'll enjoy the excitement of living in another culture. You'll find it easy to make friends with your new neighbors—native as well as North American—and you'll have adventures exploring scenic coasts, mountains, forests and picturesque villages.

Central American Retirement

To a person who hates winter and who loves foreign living, the Central American countries of Guatemala and Costa Rica are extremely attractive. From the age of 18, when my parents retired in Mexico, I spent every winter possible enjoying that country's sunny warmth and charming tropical beaches. Then in 1973, I discovered Central America during a three-month vacation through Guatemala, Honduras, El Salvador, Nicaragua and finally Costa Rica. Thus began an ongoing love affair with Central America.

Until recently, the term "Central America" carried images of civil war and dangerous traveling. Travel there was only for the most adventurous. El Salvador, Nicaragua and Guatemala made newspaper headlines and daily coverage on the six-o'clock news. Finally, after years of strife, peace has returned to most of Central America. With the return of peace and safe traveling, also comes a flood of tourists and—in Guatemala and Costa Rica—retirees.

It's difficult to know for certain how many U.S. and Canadian citizens have retired in Central America, probably close to 30,000. The majority live in Costa Rica, and a growing number are choosing Guatemala for retirement. My wife and I have joined this wave of retirement; we bought a condominium in a suburb of San José, Costa Rica, and are in the process of constructing an inexpensive house near the beach on Costa Rica's Pacific coast.

Costa Rica

Costa Rica avoided the civil/military strife that mired her sister republics in a quicksand of turmoil and tragedy. It alone remained a bastion of peaceful tranquility and a haven for American retirees. Costa Rica's devotion to democracy and peaceful cooperation with its neighbors helped it to retain its enviable position as a showcase of prosperity, respect for law and personal freedom. Partly because of this tradition of peace and democracy, partly because of the beautiful mountain ranges, Costa Rica is called "the Switzerland of the Americas." Of all foreign countries, Costa Rica has the highest percentage of North Americans living within its boundaries.

The climate here is one of the best in the world; you can choose between a year-round spring climate in the Central Plateau or a lush tropical beach climate along the Pacific and Caribbean coasts. About half the country's population lives in the center of the country, in the temperate highlands. From here, a 90-minute drive to the west takes you to the Pacific Ocean or 90 minutes east to the Caribbean. Take your pick.

Nature lovers journey here from all over the world to enjoy rain forests, cloud forests and abundant wildlife, as well as gorgeous beaches and world-class ocean fishing. Costa Rica isn't the only place with these attractions, but it's just about the only place where you can see them and feel safe. You needn't worry about being caught in a cross-fire between soldiers and rebels.

As a matter of fact, Costa Rica doesn't have any soldiers. It abolished its army 50 years ago, thus avoiding the plague of most Latin American countries: military dictatorships. Money that would normally be squandered on corruption and funneled into the Swiss bank accounts of high-ranking colonels, is spent on schools, hospitals and roads. Being a military-free zone and having a large middle class are major reasons for the country's exceptionally high standard of living.

Inflation climbed slowly here over the past few years, with the ratio of the dollar to Costa Rica's colón following suit. At this point in time, the colón trades at about 180 to the dollar. As prices go up, the number of colónes we receive for the dollar goes up as well, which keeps prices fairly steady for those with dollars in our bank accounts. The colón floats according to a free market and is not government-controlled as it is in Mexico.

Retirement on a shoestring in Costa Rica is possible, since the average U.S. Social Security check is much more than the average middle-class Costa Rican earns. The income requirement for becoming a pensionado in Costa Rica is $600 a month in pension. And, it's entirely possible to get by on this amount. A $600 paycheck is considered a good income for most Costa Rican families. However, again I caution against living in a foreign country without adequate funds. It would be extremely unwise to try living here if you had no backup resources and if $600 was all you could count on.

To give you an idea of prices in Costa Rica, our basic phone bill is less than $5 a month, and that includes almost unlimited local calls. Our electric bill rarely tops $13 a month, because our condo has neither furnace nor air conditioning. We don't need it; it never gets hot, and it never gets cold. Groceries are generally less than back home, with imported goods expensive and local produce cheap. Where you can really save is on medical costs. The most expensive

hospital room in town—in a modern, well-equipped facility—will set you back $76. That's for a private room, with
bath, telephone, TV and an extra bed for family members if
they wish to stay overnight. For about $50 a month, retirees
can buy into the Costa Rica medical system; that's everything fully covered.

Most North Americans will say that one of the best parts
about living in Costa Rica is its friendly citizens. This is an
egalitarian country; the people are outgoing, happy and
sincerely like North Americans because we are so much
like them.

Tourists are restricted to 90 days at a time in Costa Rica,
but that's long enough to get the flavor of living here and
to decide if it's an appropriate place for retirement. In San
José, where most retirees live, or at least start out living,
you might rent one of the many apartments that are available by the week or month to get the essence of the country. Becoming a retiree here requires a lot of red tape and
visits to various government ministries and rubber stamps
marking everything in sight. It's best to hire a specialist to
take care of things for you.

However, it really isn't necessary to go for pensionado
status unless you plan on living in Costa Rica full time.
Many foreigners (like my wife and I) prefer to stay the
three months allowed on a tourist permit and then go to a
beach resort just across the border in Nicaragua. After a 72-
hour stay in a very inexpensive hotel, you can return for
another three months. (We rarely stay more than three
months anyway.) Presently, the government is tolerant of
those who over-stay their visa. There's a nominal fine of
$50 plus about $5 for each month over the 90 days.
However, that could change at any moment.

My friends claim I tend to be uncritical about places I
like, stressing the upbeat and minimizing the downbeat. So
be aware that Costa Rica (as well as the other foreign countries mentioned here) are, after all, third-world nations.
Roads are not up to our standards, bureaucracy is mad-
dening, and there is crime. Central America has some of the
most highly-skilled pickpockets in the world. Burglaries,

while not as prevalent as in the United States, are more often focused on affluent foreigners. But you'll not likely escape the threat of crime by staying home, not unless you live in a particularly safe part of the United States. The best approach in Costa Rica is to be careful of your wallet in crowds and live in an area where neighbors will watch your house when you're gone.

Check your library for the latest edition of my book *Choose Costa Rica* for complete details about living, investing and retiring in Costa Rica. If the librarian doesn't have it, scold her harshly and demand that she order a copy.

Guatemala

With peace settling in over the region, Guatemala is once more becoming a practical place for retirement. Of all the economical retirement styles described in this book, Guatemala has to be the bottom line of shoestring economics. An indication of this is that the government only requires a monthly income of $300 in order to obtain a pensionado or retiree resident visa. The astounding thing is, if need be, you can actually live on $300 a month! At least 1,500 U.S. citizens and an undetermined number of Canadians have chosen retirement in Guatemala.

For shoestring retirement, I can't imagine anyplace being better than Guatemala. To get an idea of what it costs to live here, I interviewed a retired couple who live in the mountains near Guatemala City. The husband took an early retirement from his job in the United States, and they came to Guatemala to look things over. They fell in love with the country, bought a home and settled into retirement. What about costs?

"My company pension is less than $1,100. That covers all our household expenses, including two full-time maids. We also send two children to school...pay for their clothes, books and tuition plus a few dollars to their families so they won't take the kids out of school and make them work. And, I put $300 in our savings account every month."

One resident of Lake Atitlán was quoted in the Costa Rican *Tico Times* as saying, "A retired professor from the States doesn't enjoy a monumental pension, but here I can live like a maharaja, whereas in the States I'd be cashing in Green Stamps."

Gringos tend to congregate in just a few places here. Two favorite retirement sites are the old colonial city of Antigua and, on the shore of beautiful Lake Atitlán, an Indian town called Panajachel. A couple of places around the perimeter of Guatemala City are also suitable for gracious retirement living: the suburbs of San Cristóbal and Vista Hermosa. Guatemala City itself is a place to avoid. The streets are filled with litter and pickpockets.

Many long-time retirees here maintain that living in Guatemala is no more dangerous than many places in the United States. Even though political strife and civil unrest has been the rule for years, it was all but invisible to foreign residents. As one resident said, "Yes, there were terrible things happening here, but if we didn't read about it in Newsweek or Time, we'd never know about it." Another man told a reporter from the English-language newspaper Tico Times, "Being Gringos, we're pretty much protected. It doesn't serve anyone's purpose to alienate the U.S." A lady retiree said, "Really, I feel safer here in Guatemala than I would in Chicago or New York. Much safer."

I'm convinced this is true, however I must say that there are very few places in this world where I would not feel safer than in Chicago or New York! Beirut, Baghdad or Newark perhaps. Despite optimistic reports, some places in Guatemala should be definitely off limits for Gringos. During research trips for my book *Choose Costa Rica* (which includes a section on Guatemala), I admit that I strayed into some country not recommended for tourist travel, and I encountered no problems. But I don't recommend it. The problem is that the peace process is still underway; the rebels in some back-country areas are still armed. If you stick with the tourist areas and the places where North Americans retire, you'll not likely find any problems.

Study-Retirement Programs

One way of visiting Guatemala and trying it out is to attend one of the language schools there, studying Spanish. Not only is this a fascinating way of learning more about the country, but it is incredibly inexpensive. In Antigua, the location of many Spanish schools, room and board with a Guatemalan family can be arranged for $30 to $40 a week (that's $120 to $160 a month!). Schools provide one-on-one teaching for as little as $2 an hour.

One couple wanted to visit Guatemala and learn Spanish, but they decided to take their motorhome and use it for accommodations rather than stay with a Guatemalan family. Scott and Karen Bonis reported their experiences in Escapees Newsletter as follows:

"When we decided to go to a language school, we selected Projecto Linguistico Francisco Marroquín in Antigua. It is more expensive than others in the area, but it is where the U.S. Government sends its employees. You enroll by the week, so if it is not to your liking, you can change.

"The school is run by Pamela, a no-nonsense British expatriate, about 50 years old, who is a mother figure to nearly every Gringo staying in town. She can solve most problems, from finding a place to stay to changing money (at a better rate than at the border). As a result, her office is a steady parade of people.

"We entered Guatemala with 30-day entry permits for ourselves and our vehicles. The standard procedure is to get extensions of the papers which requires a trip to Guatemala City. However, there are people who specialize in obtaining tourist papers for the beleaguered tourist.

"Our school consisted of four buildings scattered throughout the town, most of which were formerly homes of wealthy families. Students work one-on-one with a teacher, and one student-teacher pair occupies each room. The room contains one small table, two wooden chairs and a 40-watt light bulb. The windows, in general, do not have glass, but rather shutters and the requisite iron bars to prevent intruders.

"School occupied the majority of our waking hours. We attended seven hours a day, five days a week, with a two-hour break for lunch. We were so saturated with Spanish that studying at the break was impossible. At night we did a few chores, rushed home to dinner, and then studied.

"At first, the teachers spoke slowly and distinctly to us. By the time we left, they were speaking at nearly normal speed and we were really grasping their thoughts. It was truly amazing how much clearer all of the native people were speaking compared to how they used to speak when we arrived just two months before!

"We don't regret it for a minute. We learned an incredible amount of Spanish, however, it is only a beginning and we surely need to study further so, yes, we will go back." (With permission from *Escapees Newsletter*, Sep.-Oct. 1991.)

Retirement in Mexico

Ten years ago, Don Merwin and I co-authored a book, *Choose Mexico*, which described how to retire in that country on a monthly expenditure of $400 a month. This fantastically low budget even allowed for servants and travel about the country! Mexico was a true paradise for "shoestring" retirement.

Although the cost of goods and services in Mexico rose steadily over the years since we wrote our first edition, for a long while the rate of exchange (the number of pesos we got for our dollars) increased accordingly. Therefore, for many years, retirees with dollars in their pockets weren't affected by inflation. The higher the prices, the more pesos they received for their dollars.

Then the Mexican government decided to control the exchange rate arbitrarily. Prices in pesos were still rising rapidly, but we weren't getting correspondingly more pesos for our dollars anymore, so North American retirees gradually lost purchasing power. Pesos became overvalued, dollars became cheap.

Our estimate of the cost of comfortable Mexican retirement rose to $600, then to $800 a month. By the end of 1994, many things in Mexico were nearly as expensive as in the

United States. Hotels which formerly cost $25 a night rose to $65. The $5 meal became $12.

For a long while, despite inflated costs, many retirees found they could still live on the equivalent of Social Security in a style far above what they could hope for at home. But the steady loss of the dollar's purchasing power began to look ominous for retirees who needed to live on a strict budget. The $400-a-month days looked like history.

Suddenly, in December 1994, the overvalued peso collapsed and fell toward a more sane level. The dollar increased its value 40 percent overnight. By March 1995, the peso was hovering around seven to the dollar, which meant retirees' dollars bought more than twice as much as they did before the peso's devaluation. An apartment which rented for 1,360 pesos a month (or $400) before December, still rented for 1,360 pesos in March, but this amounted to only an affordable $181. A meal in a nice restaurant which formerly cost $12 worth of pesos, now cost $5.50. Unless things change radically (and it doesn't look like they will anytime soon), the halcyon days of $400-a-month retirement are back! This is exciting news for those wishing to combine interesting foreign retirement with a shoestring budget.

What can you do with $400 today? It's possible to rent a two-bedroom apartment, eat well (including dining out at least once a week at a nice restaurant), and even hire a cleaning lady one day a week to take care of the house and do the laundry. One thing that makes this possible is that you don't need to spend money on heating. If that isn't enough, this budget even covers medical insurance.

My co-author and I take turns every so often spending a month or so in Mexico in order to update *Choose Mexico*. During our last visit, my wife and I traveled to a popular retirement area, rented an apartment for a month and kept scrupulous track of our expenditures. (Note that this was before the devaluation.) We found that a basic monthly budget would come under $800. By this year's peso exchange rate, however, that budget would be $350 a month!

In one respect, year-round retirement here isn't as easy as it used to be, either. The Mexican government raised the minimum income requirement you need to obtain a resident permit and become a full-time resident. Time was, you needed just $550 a month in retirement income; today it's up to $2,200 (this is, of course, subject to change). But that's no problem for most retirees since tourist visas are good for six months at a time. You simply make a trip up to the border every half a year, do some heavy-duty shopping and return for another six months. A huge number of retirees don't want to live in Mexico full time anyway. They prefer to spend November through March enjoying the sunny weather here, and then return to enjoy the best part of the year at home.

A few notes on driving in Mexico: most Mexican highways are adequately paved, but not designed for high-speed driving. Mexican drivers tend to drive slowly; they seem to believe that the slower they drive, the longer their vehicles will last. It's best to fall back into this mode, because we shouldn't be tearing up the highways anyway. The worst thing about Mexican highways is that they lack wide shoulders. Often, roads have no shoulders at all. This is fine for driving during the daytime, but not at night. Never drive at night! The roads are poorly lit and a surprise collision with an enormous brahma bull can be deadly for you as well as for the animal.

An even more important piece of driving advice is never drive in Mexico without Mexican automobile insurance. Non-Mexican insurance is not valid. Fortunately, insurance is inexpensive if you buy from the right source. (Don't believe the guidebooks when they say all Mexican insurance costs the same.) Details on insurance and other essentials can be found in my book *RV Travel in Mexico*, which I suggest you check out at your library.

Where North Americans Live

We've discussed RV retirement in Mexico during the winter. But spending a summer in Baja California would be only slightly less uncomfortable than spending a summer in a pizza oven. The Mexican mainland is where most North Americans choose conventional retirement living.

Mexico is a large country, with an amazing variety of climates, landscapes and panoramas. From tropical Pacific beaches to high, snow-clad mountains, you can find any type of lifestyle imaginable in Mexico. However, unless you are fluent in Spanish, you'll probably want to try your retirement in a place where other North Americans can keep you company. That isn't because Mexicans aren't friendly; it's simply because you'd soon become bored silly with no one to communicate with.

So if you're looking for company, one place to go is to Guadalajara and its environs. More than 30,000 North Americans call this home. Between the city and the many small communities clustered around Lake Chapala, you'll find a wide assortment of English-speaking groups where you will be accepted as friends. Helping newcomers get their start in Mexico is part of the tradition here.

Guadalajara is in the temperate highlands, a location the residents like to describe as a "place of perpetual spring." Others prefer the tropics, romantic places like Acapulco, Puerto Vallarta or Mazatlán. Even though these places have a deserved reputation as expensive, jet-set resorts, you'll discover that the North American retirees enjoy life on a different level: less expensive and less hectic. Although retiring in one of these communities on less than Social Security is entirely possible, it's best to figure on a little more.

Many locations in Mexico make wonderful places to retire, too many to be described here in a few paragraphs. From Baja to the Yucatán Peninsula, retirement locations are described in the book *Choose Mexico*. Most libraries have a copy, so before you make any decisions, check it out.

Is Mexico Safe?

This frequently-asked question is frustrating to anyone who has traveled in Mexico to any extent. The misinformation and distorted pictures of Mexico that most folks carry in their minds are difficult to dispel without actually taking a trip into Mexico. The truth is, Mexican people are gentle, polite and extremely law-abiding. Oh, that our society could be as law-abiding as theirs! Why? One reason is that the law there is very strict and tough on habitual criminals. Upon the third conviction, a criminal automatically receives a 20-year sentence. This discourages people from becoming criminals, as you can well imagine. People who go to Mexico often will tell you that they have no fear of walking the streets of an average Mexican town at any time, day or night. That's not to say Mexico doesn't have its share of crime, particularly in bigger cities; as anywhere in the world, the larger the city, the more crime.

I've heard many horror stories over the years about someone's brother-in-law's friend who had difficulties with the police when involved in a minor accident. Yet, during my years of driving in Mexico (nearly 100,000 miles), I've never been unfairly hassled by police. I've interviewed many Americans who've been involved in accidents in Mexico, and they've had nothing but praise for their insurance companies and the local authorities.

In an issue of Loners on Wheels Newsletter, a retired single lady, driving her motorhome toward Cancun, Mexico, described an accident this way: "Two days into Mexico, like a turkey, I stopped for a feathered turkey sitting in the road. A big truck loaded with oranges didn't stop. The trucker's insurance paid for my damages. It's strictly against the law in Mexico to hit anyone stopped on the road! The police and my insurance adjuster couldn't have been nicer. Two days later, the garage had miraculously patched up my RV, so my trip continued."

I'm sure bad things happen in Mexico, just as they can occur anywhere. Yet, I'm personally convinced that the incidents are fewer and farther between than here. One point that needs to be made, however: do not confuse the mordida (bite) that a police officer accepts with a bribe. If you speed, if you go through a stop light or stop sign, and a cop sees you, he will give you a ticket, just as will a cop in Toronto or Toledo. The difference is, you can pay the fine to the cop and avoid having him take your license plates (if he did take your plates, you'd have to pay the ticket at the police station to retrieve your plates—very inconvenient). This money is considered part of the cop's pay, and he is doing you a favor by taking it. However don't, under any circumstance, give a mordida if you are innocent. Doing so will only encourage inventing "traffic offenses." Insist on a ticket and pay at the police station; that way the cop won't get any money. Believe me, most of the time a patrolman stops you in Mexico, you've done something wrong. So, bargain for the amount of the fine and let it go at that.

The Peace Corps

For foreign retirement on a shoestring, here's the best option of all: join the Peace Corps! It isn't as crazy as it might seem at first glance. The Peace Corps actively seeks out older, retired citizens who have much to contribute. No other group in this country embodies the years of leadership, skills, experience and proven ability of our senior citizens. For the first time in their lives many senior citizens find themselves without commitments to a career or family, and they are finding fulfillment and excitement in the job of helping others. In addition, they're getting paid for it! They're having the time of their lives, and at the same time participating in programs that affect literacy, health, hunger and help promote world peace, friendship and sharing. Retired singles and couples have put their expertise to work in Africa, Asia, South America, Central America and the Pacific Islands.

Peace Corps volunteers receive living expenses and a monthly stipend to cover incidental needs, so there is no need for them to spend savings or other income. In addition, a monthly payment is put aside and given to them at the end of the typical two-year assignment. This severance pay comes in handy for making a transition back into life at home. The compensation you receive from the Peace Corps doesn't affect your Social Security earnings. Since all expenses are paid, many older Peace Corps volunteers bank their entire Social Security, pension and interest income during their two-year tour of duty.

Here is a terrific opportunity to make a contribution to peace, to utilize your life's experience helping others, and to have the time of your life. If you're married, odds are that your spouse also has some much-needed skill, so there's a chance that the two of you might go overseas as a team. For further information or an application, write to Peace Corps, Room P-301, Washington, DC 20526; or call (800) 424-8580.

Chapter Thirteen

Our Favorite Retirement Places

When someone suggested that we list our favorite retirement locations, it sounded easy. After all, my wife and I have visited and inspected many, many parts of the country in the course of our research travels. However, when we sat down to compile our list, we discovered that we had to choose from a list of almost 300 nice places we had visited over the past 13 years of retirement explorations.

We found it next to impossible to choose just a few favorites. We missed too many desirable retirement havens by restricting our list to specific towns or cities. Often, three or four places are clustered in a general area: areas like the Carolina coastlines, California's Gold Country or the Rio Grande Valley in Texas. Therefore, we organized our list into places—sometimes clustered around a single town, sometimes scattered over an entire region.

Compiling this list of favorite retirement places made us even more aware of the subjective nature of what constitutes a "good" place to live. Between ourselves, my wife and I argued and discussed each location as to whether it should be included or ignored as a possible retirement site. Many otherwise great places were eliminated because of economics. It wasn't easy, but we've never claimed that finding a retirement haven is an easy task.

Because we agree that these possibilities presented here might suit our retirement needs, that doesn't necessarily mean they would be suitable for everyone. If you want more information, all of these places, plus the ones we eliminated from the list, are described in greater detail in my book *Where To Retire*.

Alabama

Dothan—Quality real estate is quite affordable in this popular retirement location in southern Alabama, about 90 minutes from Florida's beaches. There's a cosmopolitan makeup to the local citizens; they come from all over the country, not just from the Deep South. Dothan is the commercial center of the area, with the smaller cities of Ozark and Enterprise part of the complex of desirable neighborhoods. A large percentage of new retirees are ex-military. Property taxes are exceptionally low, as is the cost of living.

Scottsboro—Situated in the northern part of the state, Scottsboro is a picture-book version of a retirement town. An antique courthouse and old-fashioned town square, tree-graced neighborhoods of substantial brick homes, reasonable housing and lakes galore, all contribute to making this a pleasant community for retirement. Scottsboro sits on one of the Southeast's largest lake complexes (Guntersville Lake), with over a thousand miles of shoreline. Even though its population is only about 15,000, Scottsboro has ample shopping and facilities and is a short drive from larger cities.

Arizona

Ajo/Bisbee—These are two western mining towns that drew bargain-hunting retirees when large mining corporations suddenly closed down operations, sending the towns into economic tailspins. Property values dropped to almost giveaway prices. The towns worked very hard to change their images and attract retirees to take up the slack. This plan worked admirably, with retirement replacing mining as the major industry. Real estate prices recovered to some extent, but prices are still bargain-basement attractive. A welcoming attitude on the part of residents and town officials makes Bisbee and Ajo places worth investigating.

Lake Havasu City/Parker/Bullhead City—These low-desert retirement towns on the banks of the Colorado River offer great real estate bargains. Hot in the summer, but

pleasantly warm and dry in the winter, the area loses population when the Snowbirds fly north in late April.
Laughlin—just across the river from Bullhead City—is one
of the fastest-growing casino complexes in Southern
Nevada. Casino restaurants compete for customers with
low-cost specials like $5 prime rib dinners and rows of
nickle slot machines to lure away your shoestring bankroll.

Arkansas

Bull Shoals/Mountain Home/Lakeview—This area
offers real estate bargains and reasonable living costs.
Added attractions are friendly neighbors, good fishing and
lovely scenery. Traditional retirement areas like California
and Florida are losing retirees who move here to take
advantage of an exceptionally low crime rate and gorgeous
scenery. Surrounded on three sides by water, Bull Shoals
and Lakeview sit on the shore of a lake that stretches for
almost 100 miles. Its deep, blue waters are legend among
bass fishermen, and the rivers and streams feeding the lake
are considered premier for rainbow trout fishing, which in
the spring and summer is often done at night under lights.

Eureka Springs—Here's a most unusual Ozark mountain town, well-preserved, looking much as it did 100 years
ago, and famous for its hot springs and lovely Victorian
homes, many at bargain prices. A relatively mild, four-season climate makes this an ideal retirement area. Not too far
away is Fayetteville, a college town with a surprisingly rich
cultural atmosphere. This area supports lots of city services
yet is only a short distance from hunting, fishing and all
that goes with outdoor sports in the beautiful Ozarks.

Heber Springs—About 60 miles north of Little Rock,
Heber Springs and Greers Ferry draw many retirees who
love fishing. The towns overlook a 40,000-acre lake with
300 miles of wooded shoreline and waters overrun with
bass, stripers, wall eye, catfish and lunker-sized trout. This
is one of the few places in the country where it's possible to
fish for bass, wall eye and trout in the same day.
Inexpensive property, low taxes, a temperate climate and

an almost non-existent crime rate add to the attraction of retirement here.

California

Burney/Fall River Mills—Tucked away in California's northern mountains are two little-known, lovely retirement gems. Outdoor recreation is year-round and property is inexpensive. The highway east from Redding winds past several abandoned mines as it makes its way to the towns of Burney and Fall River Mills. Today, gold mining is no longer an economic force, having been pushed aside by wild-rice farming in Fall River, lumber mills in Burney. Choose from deep, cold lakes or mountain streams for bass and trout; try the warmer waters for catfish and crappie. Lakes Britton, Eastman, Fall River, Baum Crystal and Iron Canyon are a lure to all types of fishermen. With a short drive to the northwest, fishermen will find other hot spots on Bear Creek, Medicine Lake, McCloud River and others.

Dunsmuir—Clinging to the banks of the Sacramento River as it wends its way through a narrow canyon, the town of Dunsmuir offers an outdoor wonderland and rustic old homes at bargain prices. The town enjoys a spectacular view of snow-covered Mt. Shasta in the distance. This ancient volcano, 14,110 feet high, is one of the highest peaks on the continent and offers some pretty fair skiing at a place called Snowman's Hill. The area is famous for trout, sometimes large native ones, that tempt the fisherman to the shores of the Sacramento River.

Eureka/Fort Bragg/Mendocino—Along California's rugged northern coasts you'll find a string of picturesque villages offering quality retirement. The towns are small, neighborly and uncrowded, sitting along the coast, interspersed with forest and grazing land, sleepy and laid-back just as they should be. Small, family-owned wineries and artist galleries attract tourists. Housing costs are moderate If you are looking for discos, beach parties and tourist traps, you are much too far north. If you hate hot summers and abhor cold winters, this is place. Frost is all but unheard of, with 40 degrees just about as cold as it ever gets in January. Highs in January—in Eureka, for example—average 53 degrees, but the July and August highs rarely top 70 degrees!

California Gold Rush Country—Angels Camp, Fiddletown, Calaveras and a host of other boomtowns of the '49er days attract tourists and retirees alike. These picturesque locations not only offer historical ambience, but also reasonable housing prices and easy access to outdoor sports. A 90-minute drive, or less, takes you skiing in the high Sierras, gaming in Reno or Lake Tahoe, or to the lights of San Francisco. A four-season climate brings occasional light snows in the winter and gorgeous spring and fall weather. There's still some gold in these hills, with weekend panning for nuggets a favorite retiree hobby.

Yucaipa—Midway between Palm Springs and Los Angeles is an excellent example of high-desert living. With an altitude higher than either of those places, Yucaipa enjoys cooler summers than nearby Palm Springs. With 25 inches of rain a year, the countryside is considerably greener than much of the nearby country as well. In fact, the word "yucaipa" is supposed to have come from a Serrano Indian word meaning "wet, green place." Inexpensive mobile home parks here make cutting living costs easier. On the eastern and northern edges of the community the mountains rise to over a mile high, up to the ski country of Big Bear and Lake Arrowhead.

Colorado

Grand Junction—The economy here suffered terribly when the oil shale boom collapsed in the 1980s. Real estate dropped to unbelievably low levels. Today the area has made a nice recovery, largely due to local businesses actively campaigning for retirees to settle there. In Grand Junction and nearby towns, housing is quite affordable. Shopping malls, a senior citizens' center and excellent health care are among the attractions. An abundance of sunshine and a mild winter that permits golf and tennis to be year-round sports adds to the area's attraction as a retirement center.

Florida

Those who think Florida is expensive may have a surprise coming. Parts of this state offer some of the best retirement bargains, dollar for dollar and feature for feature, of anywhere in the country. You can find housing costs that are lower in places like Oklahoma or Idaho, but winter heating bills cancel out this advantage.

Daytona Beach/St. Augustine—Daytona is divided into two sectors: one for tourists—on the peninsula's ocean side—and the mainland for ordinary residents. Retirees can find reasonable-to-cheap accommodations away from the beach, a short drive away. The 23-mile-long white sand beach is perhaps Daytona's most famous feature, one of the few places in Florida where autos are permitted to drive along the shore. Besides good beaches and pleasant winters, excellent senior citizen services add to the value of retirement here.

Fort Walton Beach/Panama City/Pensacola—Between Panama City and Pensacola you'll find a selection of towns ranging from ordinary to luxurious (on a small scale of luxury). An interesting area for retirement is on a body of water known as Choctawhatchee Bay. This is the self-styled "Emerald Coast." It includes the town of Navarre and a dozen other small places. The entire stretch of coast offers good fishing and beach recreation and fairly reasonable living costs, particularly in the off-season. It's hotter here in the summer and cooler in the winter than southern Florida, however.

Ocala/Orlando—Inland Florida is quite rural once away from the metropolitan districts. Farms and acreage are priced less than one might expect. Also, just east of the Tampa-St. Petersburg area is a semi-rural area where very affordable real estate and inexpensive mobile-home living make for true shoestring retirement. Anywhere in west Florida can be considerably less expensive than the "Gold

Coast" glitter around Miami. There are some excellent buys in homes, both in new developments and older, settled neighborhoods. An advantage to living in central Florida is your proximity to beaches; it's about an hour drive to either coast for beach fun.

Georgia

Rabun County/Clayton—Clayton is the largest town in Rabun County, in fact it's the only settlement worthy of being called much more than a village. For this reason, folks hereabouts don't think in terms of towns; when you ask where they live, they'll reply "Rabun County," rather than mention a specific locality. Clayton is the commercial center for the county's 11,648 residents; as such, it provides a good selection of shopping, business and medical services. Two hospitals with 24-hour emergency rooms deliver a wide range of health care services. One feature all residents point to proudly is their four-season weather. As local boosters say, "This is where spring spends the summer."

Valdosta—Valdosta is set in Georgia's "Plantation Trace," a region marked by fertile plains, bountiful woods and hundreds of blue lakes. Steeped in Victorian history and architecture, as well as modern subdivisions, Valdosta stands out as south Georgia's dominant city. Immaculately maintained neighborhoods, shaded by enormous trees, make Valdosta's residential sections exceptionally inviting. Moody Air Force Base is responsible for many military retirees choosing retirement here. Coming from all over the nation, they add to the cosmopolitan makeup of the retiree population. Not far from the Florida state line, Valdosta is a short drive to Florida's beaches.

Kentucky

Bowling Green—A living stereotype of Kentucky, complete with bluegrass, thoroughbreds and friendly neighbors, Bowling Green is attracting retirees from more northerly states. It's a small city, not big enough to suffer from big-city problems. Crime rates are exceptionally low, pollution is almost non-existent and the cost of living is 10 percent below national average. Housing and utility costs are low, with homes selling for 17 percent below average and utilities at an astounding 27 percent less than national averages. Another factor in maintaining an upscale atmosphere is the presence of Western Kentucky University, with 15,000 students adding intellectual warmth.

Murray—This small city consistently garners recommendations from retirement writers as a good place to relocate. Murray is an excellent example of how good things happen to a community when retirees move in. When 250 couples retired here because of favorable publicity, the extra retirees were enough to push the city into enlarging the senior citizens' center and adding more services. The staff at the local center, by the way, is dedicated and enthusiastic about plans for the facility's future. Real estate prices have risen somewhat, but are still reasonable.

Louisiana

Baton Rouge—A university town, with an intellectual atmosphere and retirees from all parts of the country, Baton Rouge consistently registers one of the lowest costs of living of any city of its size in the nation. Living costs are still almost seven percent below average, so Baton Rouge remains an affordable retirement option. It is, however, a large city (250,000 population) with some of the attendant woes. Many smaller towns within a short drive might be worth investigating for your retirement.

Cajun Country—West and south of Baton Rouge is "Cajun Country," the most famous part of Louisiana. At one time, Cajuns were noted for their closed society. As a defense mechanism, they jealously maintained their French language and their private ways of living. Times have changed, thanks to television, modern transportation and open communications, however. Retirees are welcome, and living is easy in this charming region. This area is for folks who like "country," who fit into a down-home atmosphere and who relish crawfish gumbo.

Houma—Small cities such as Houma, about 75 miles southwest of New Orleans, always report an unusually low incidence of crime. This typical Louisiana small town may not be appropriate for Northerners who aren't used to the nuances of the rural South, but the people are always friendly. Leesville, to the north, is another small town, but with a large military influence, which attracts retirees from other parts of the country.

Mississippi

One of the states which is actively seeking retirees to relocate, Mississippi recently passed legislation exempting all pensions from state income taxes. Oxford was described in the chapter on education and retirement. Other towns worth investigating are Columbus, an old-style southern city, and Hattiesburg, a city of 49,000 population 90 minutes from the Gulf.

Gulfport-Biloxi—A string of pleasant retirement communities here attract Northerners and military retirees because of their pleasant ambience and low housing costs. Housing has risen considerably, however, since the advent of gambling casinos in the twin cities of Gulfport and Biloxi. This industry created 5,000 new jobs, bringing workers into the area to compete for homes. Gambling also tarnished the pristine retiree image somewhat, so now the best places to retire are in smaller towns, away from the tourist and gambling action, places like Bay St. Louis, Long Beach or Pass Christian.

Missouri

Lake of the Ozarks—This is the center of a network of small, picturesque towns in the Missouri Ozarks, which are ideal for those seeking a recreation-filled retirement. Housing costs are competitive and good highways take residents to St. Louis for heavy-duty shopping. The Lake of the Ozarks area is a major commercial center, providing good shopping, restaurants and entertainment. Other areas are more rural and isolated, in rustic Ozark settings. Here, you'll find small farms that cost less than a new car. If you've always wanted to try farming as a hobby, this might be the place to go.

Nevada

Las Vegas/Reno—Local casinos here make it a point to hire senior citizens as part-time workers. Although the cost of living is not low, employment opportunities and gambling excitement make it worthwhile for some. Competition between casinos forces them to offer tremendous values in restaurant food and entertainment, which makes "going out" easy on a shoestring budget.

New Mexico

Albuquerque—Dry weather and a university-assisted cultural climate, combined with a reasonable cost of living, make Albuquerque a favorite. Neighborhoods are neat, shopping is excellent and the downtown area is user-friendly. Some recommended residential areas are near the university, which affords many cultural activities at little or no cost to senior citizens.

Carlsbad/Las Cruces—Carlsbad is a small city that actively encourages retirees to relocate. The local chamber of commerce is very helpful. Carlsbad's main drawback is its location so far from the closest metropolitan area: El Paso. Other economical New Mexico towns are Las Cruces and Truth or Consequences. Las Cruces is closer to El Paso; Truth or Consequences, closer to Albuquerque.

North Carolina

We're convinced that some of the most beautiful and scenic places in the world are found in the Blue Ridge and

Great Smokey mountains. October, when leaves are turning, is a marvelous time for a visit. Hardwood trees display a full explosion of color, with brilliant reds, yellows, purples and lavenders, and all colors in between, to dazzle the eye while evergreens provide a conservative background of green. We've also made the rounds in the spring, when the dogwoods, azaleas and mountain laurel trees are in full bloom.

Asheville—The population center of the area, with a university adding intellectual vigor to the surroundings, Asheville is conveniently located in the Appalachian foothills to many outdoor recreation opportunities. Nearby Hendersonville and Brevard also have received high ratings for retirement possibilities.

Blowing Rock/Boone/Newland—These gorgeous settings in the Great Smokey Mountains draw many retirees in search of milder summers and picturesque winters. Living costs here range from very low to very high, so shopping around is recommended.

Oklahoma

Grand Lake o' the Cherokees/Tenkiller—Part of a large network of lakes on the fringes of the Ozark Mountains, some of the nation's cheapest real estate is found here, tucked away amongst picturesque forests, Ozark hills and unsophisticated small towns. The Grand Lake is large enough for good-sized sailboats and permits private boat docks (which many waterways the Army Corps of Engineers manages usually prohibit). Some areas, however, are only for those of you with hermit tendencies. Not far away is the city of Bartlesville, a contrast in city living, yet with Oklahoma hospitality and affordable living.

Oregon

Ashland/Medford/Grants Pass/Eugene—These inland valley cities, with quality living, access to outdoor sports and low housing costs make these towns popular with

California retirees. The winters are mild, with very little snow, and the surroundings are green year-round. Despite Oregon's reputation for rain, this area receives about half the precipitation of most Eastern and Midwestern cities, but without the oppressive freezing weather.

Oregon Coast—All along the coast, interspersed between beaches and cliffs, are places such as Brookings, Coos Bay, Florence, Gold Beach and Port Orford. The weather here is one of the mildest in the nation, with almost no frost and rarely any days over 79 degrees. Residents refer to the area as Oregon's "banana belt." There's some justification, since flowers bloom all year locally. Real estate is bargain-priced. Just across the border from California are the twin towns of Brookings and Harbor. An estimated 30 percent of their population are retirees.

South Carolina

Aiken—A lovely Deep South city, where a mixture of Northern and Southern retirees take full advantage of retirement opportunities. Aiken is a candidate for retirement relocation for a number of reasons, not the least of which is its beautiful, gracious setting. Huge antebellum mansions and cute little cottages are shaded by enormous trees on meticulously landscaped lots. Aiken's robust business district makes it look larger than it actually is, because it's the shopping and employment center for a large area. It recently received praise from Money Magazine as one of the better places in the country to retire.

Myrtle Beach—A summer beach resort that has lots of retirees from the North who enjoy the seashore and mild winters, this area receives consistent recommendations from retirement writers, despite a tremendous boost in tourism. Lately Myrtle Beach has been promoting a "Grand Ol' Opry" kind of development. This may put a strain on local facilities and housing costs, and it may not be the retirement Eden it once was; judge for yourself.

Tennessee

Clarksville—Because of the large military base here, this has become a popular retirement place for servicemen from all parts of the country. An exceptionally friendly population and reasonable costs are the pluses. Clarksville sits conveniently on an interstate highway that whisks you to the big city of Nashville in less than 45 minutes. This is one of our favorite Mid-Southern Hills locations. Clarksville combines an atmosphere of small-town living with city and urban conveniences. The nearby town of Dover is typical of a small Tennessee town with very inexpensive costs. Dover is becoming popular because of its proximity to the Land Between the Lakes and its outdoor recreational opportunities.

Crossville—In a rolling, wooded, agricultural country-side, Crossville is typical of many Tennessee-Kentucky mid-sized towns. Nearby Fairfield Glen attracts retirees from Michigan, Ohio and Indiana. The town is dry, with residents routinely making the trek to Knoxville for booze—a 70-mile drive each way. When I expressed dismay that drunks should be free-wheeling down the interstate for their supplies, residents cheerfully assured me that bootleggers are plentiful in Crossville. "Why, you can buy anything you want, right here!" There are several small communities near the city of Crossville that feature inexpensive, large parcels of land. Two golf-course communities nearby offer relatively moderate properties.

Texas

Austin/San Antonio—These are two of Texas' bargain spots for real estate and apartment rentals. Overbuilding has caused prices to remain stable or to drop in a market of ever-increasing costs. Mild climates and plenty of cultural activities add to the attraction. San Antonio, like Austin to the north, enjoys a low cost of living, almost 12 percent below national averages and the lowest of the 25 U.S. metro areas. Low-cost utilities and real estate are partly responsible for this happy condition. Residential areas flourish on the fringes of the city, with new subdivisions popping up everywhere. The central area and older sections have the biggest bargains in real estate, sometimes in the low $30,000s, yet you shouldn't make decisions on price alone; some areas are not suitable for the majority of retirees. Most newcomers prefer to live in the outer ring of newer subdivisions, near one of several large shopping centers.

Corpus Christi/Galveston—Both Corpus Christi and Galveston suffer from split personalities. On the one side we have seasonal tourists, and on the other side, we have residents. The trick to retiring in one of these cities is finding a home away from the tourist side. The payoff is a mild climate with great Gulf fishing and endless beaches.

El Paso/Laredo—Border towns with easy access to Mexico for shopping and recreation usually rank very low in cost of living. American modern and old Mexican charm blends to give these places a distinctive character. In El Paso, you'll find a proliferation of apartment buildings competing for tenants. Like many Texas cities that participated in the savings-and-loan jubilee, condo and apartment construction resulted in an over-supply. Some apartments offer the first month's rent free, or free utilities for the first year, maybe even color televisions to bring you into the fold. Shopping across the border in Mexico can cut costs on many items.

Rio Grande Valley—Harlingen, McAllen and Brownsville are the choice of countless part-time retirees, filling up every winter, only to become all but vacant in the summer. Those who can stand summer heat will find rock-bottom housing prices here. In addition to the sweet aroma of citrus blossoms in December, residents enjoy a particularly colorful Christmas because of the abundance of poinsettias throughout the area. The Mexican city of Reynosa sits across the river from McAllen and is a popular shopping destination. As is the case in all the border towns, tourist cards or passports aren't required for visits of less than 72 hours unless you travel to the interior of Mexico.

Utah

Cedar City/St. George—These cities are often ranked high in guides and magazines on where to retire. Real estate is moderately priced, and if you get into the more rural areas, you can find bargain housing. St. George—a few miles to the south of Cedar City, on the edge of Zion National Park—is by far the more picturesque choice, with stark red cliffs sometimes looming vertically from resident's backyards. Both places also score unusually high in personal safety. More outsiders come here to retire than in any other Utah communities, which is important for non-Mormons, because the Mormon church is very strong here.

Washington

Aberdeen—An example of a place in economic doldrums, Aberdeen has been hit by the double whammy of lumber and fishing slumps. Real estate prices and rentals are about the lowest we've seen anywhere. Many homes are selling below $30,000. The U.S. Dept. of Housing and Urban Development has converted repossessions into subsidized housing. If you can qualify, you might find very inexpensive rents. Like all Northwest locations near the ocean, Aberdeen's weather is perfect for those who hate freezing weather and hot summers. You'll never need air conditioning here. But it's boring for those who love hot sunshine and don't like winter rain.

Vancouver—Just across the Columbia River from Portland, Vancouver offers even lower housing costs even though Portland has a reputation for being quite reasonable. Vancouver's tax situation is ideal. Why? The state of Washington does not collect state income taxes, yet it provides substantial property tax relief to low-income senior citizens. However, the state does have a sales tax. Vancouver residents handle this quite well; they simply cross the Columbia River into Oregon when making major purchases, because Oregon has no sales tax! As for winter weather, you'll never need a snow shovel in Vancouver.

Appendix

Recommended Reading

Books

Howells, John. *Choose Costa Rica*, 2nd ed. (1994) Gateway Books, Oakland, CA. Long-term travel, retirement and investment in Costa Rica. A how-to book on inexpensive living in a delightful foreign country.

Howells, John. *RV Travel in Mexico*. (1989) Gateway Books, Oakland, CA. Tips on travel, where to go, how to deal with local people, plus complete listings of over 400 parks in Mexico.

Howells, John. *Where to Retire*, 2nd ed. (1995) Gateway Books, Oakland, CA. Descriptions of over 100 locations, weather and crime statistics, plus unusual retirement opportunities.

Howells, John and Merwin, Don. *Choose Mexico*, 4th ed. (1994) Gateway Books, Oakland, CA. How to retire in Mexico and have an interesting and affordable lifestyle. Descriptions of the country and tips on where to retire.

Levitin, Nancy. *Retirement Rights: The Benefits of Growing Older*. (1994) Avon Books, New York. An excellent presentation of entitlements, programs for seniors and a full range of options for the retired and about to retire, with lots of detailed information.

McMillon, Bill. *Volunteer Vacations*. (1989) Chicago Review Press, Chicago. A directory of short-term adventures that will benefit both you and others.

Peterson, Joe and Kay. *Encyclopedia for RVers*. (1992) RoVers Publications, 100 Rainbow Dr., Livingston, TX 77351; (800) 976-8377. Full of information on all aspects of RV travel as well as a complete list of services, organizations, publications and essential addresses for RV travelers.

Peterson, Kay. *Home Is Where You Park It*, 3rd ed. (1994) RoVers Publications (see address above). Manual on full-time RVing, with tips on getting started and adjusting to a new lifestyle.

Porcino, Jane. *Living Longer, Living Better: Adventures in Community Housing for Those in the Second Half of Life*. (1990) Continuum Publishing, New York.

Symons, Allene and Parker, Jane. *Adventures Abroad*. (1991) Gateway Books, Oakland, CA. First-hand descriptions of retirement living in 12 countries, with information on housing, medical care, laws, finances and security.

Helping Out in the Outdoors. American Hiking Society, 1015 31st St. NW, Washington, DC 20007. Yearly publication. Over 100 pages of volunteer opportunities throughout the country at city, county, state and national parks.

Intentional Communities: A Guide to Cooperative Living. (1991) Communities Publications Cooperative, Stelle, IL. Very complete listing of alternative housing communities.

Volunteer! (1992) Council on International Educational Exchange, 205 E. 42nd St., New York, NY 10017. A comprehensive guide to voluntary service in the U.S. and abroad.

Periodicals

Escapees Magazine. Escapees, Inc., 100 Rainbow Dr., Livingston, TX 77351; (800) 976-8377. Bimonthly publication specializing in full-time RV travelers, but full of information for any RV owner.

Successful Retirement. Grass Roots Publishing, P.O. Box 7321, Red Oak, IA 51591. Bi-monthly, focusing on retiree issues. Billed as "The Magazine to Keep You Young."

Tico Times. Dept. 717, PO Box 025216, Miami, FL 33102. Costa Rican daily newspaper in English, a must for anyone planning on retiring in this country; three-month trial subscription for $16.50.

Where to Retire. Vacation Publications, 1502 Augusta #415, Houston, TX 77057; (713) 974-6903. Features various towns and cities around the country that are suitable for retirement and discusses many issues of concern to those of retirement age.

Workamper News. 201 Hiram Rd., Heber Springs, AR 72543; (800) 446-5627. Excellent publication listing temporary and long-term jobs for RV travelers. Free employment and situation-wanted ads. A 40-page publication every other month. By subscription only, $23 a year.

Health-Care Publications

The following free publications are available from the Exec. Secretariat Office, Health Care Fin. Admin., U.S. Dept. of Health

& Human Services, 6325 Security Blvd., Baltimore, MD 21207; (410) 966-6584.

The Medicare Handbook. An all-new, comprehensive guide to Medicare. Includes a summary of new benefits and the costs to beneficiaries under the Medicare Catastrophic Coverage Act. Discusses hospital and medical insurance, applying for coverage, submitting and appealing claims, and what Medicare does and does not cover.

Medicare and You. Explains Medicare and its two parts. Describes services covered and lists those not covered.

Medicaid and You. Presents a thorough overview of the Medicaid program and how to qualify.

Medicaid Services State-by-State. Lists basic Medicaid services required by the federal government, as well as optional services provided by each state. Outlines each state's eligibility guidelines.

Guide to Health Insurance for People with Medicare. A guide to private health insurance to supplement Medicare, what type of insurance to buy to cover items Medicare doesn't pay for.

Housing Publications

The following publications are free except as noted.

Shared Housing Programs. National Shared Housing Resource Center, 6344 Greene St., Philadelphia, PA 19144; (215) 848-1220. Describes various arrangements in which two or more unrelated people pool their resources and share a dwelling, with each individual having his or her own private room, and sharing common living areas.

A Consumer's Guide to Homesharing. Published jointly by AARP and the National Shared Housing Resource Center. (See above for address.) For those thinking about sharing their homes or seeking a homesharing arrangement.

Home Equity Conversion Consumer Facts. Commission on Legal Problems of the Elderly, American Bar Association, 1800 M St. NW, Washington, DC 20036; (202) 331-2297. A $15 check (made payable to the ABA) brings you this legal look at home equity conversion, covering sale leaseback, reverse mortgages, deferred payment loans, and property tax deferral. Also lists sources for more information.

Alternatives in Retirement Living. Village House, 19310 Club House Rd., Gaithersburg, MD 20879; (301) 921-0445. This booklet assists in evaluating your needs, choosing a retirement community.

Living Independently: Housing Choices for Older People. American Association of Homes for the Aging, 1129 20th St. NW, Ste. 400, Washington, DC 20036; (202) 296-5960. Free brochure, examines the variety of housing options available to older people.

Home Equity Conversion Facts. AARP Fulfillment, 601 E St. NW, Washington, DC 20049. Free leaflet (#DII59) talks about converting the asset value of a home into cash without having to move to another residence.

Housing Choices for Older Homeowners. AARP Fulfillment, 601 E St. NW, Washington, DC 20049. This leaflet (#DI2026) discusses the advantages, disadvantages, and restraints of home equity conversion, and other options for homeowners.

The following booklets are available for a small charge from your regional Housing & Urban Development office:

Accessory Apartments: Housing Option for Older Persons (#TOP32/CEH)

Accessory Apartments: The Most Asked Questions (#TOP33/CEH)

ECHO Units: The Most Asked Questions (#TOP35/CEH)

Home Equity Conversion: Option for Older Homeowners (#TOP37/CEH)

Home Sharing: Reducing Housing Costs for Seniors (#TOP38/CEH)

Making Home Sharing Work for You (#TOP39/CEH)

Match-Up Home Sharing: The Most Asked Questions (#TOP41/CEH)

Employment Publications

AARP Senior Employment Program. AARP Fulfillment, 601 E St. NW, Washington, DC 20049. Free brochure describes Senior Community Service Employment Program (SCSEP), which offers temporary work experience for people 55 and older with limited financial resources, tells how program works and states where it's available.

Working Options: How to Plan Your Job Search, Your Work Life. AARP Workforce Educ. Sect., 601 E St. NW, Washington, DC 20049. Free booklet evaluates your work skills, checks out the job market and offers advice on how to land a job. Also lists books, employment programs, state resources, and volunteer opportunities.

After 65: Resources for Self-Reliance. Public Affairs Pamphlets, 381 Park Ave. South, New York, NY 10016; (212) 683-4331.

Pamphlet $1. Topics include: working during retirement, in-home care, meal services, senior centers and legal assistance.

Merchandising Your Job Talents. Consumer Info. Center, P.O. Box 100, Pueblo, CO 81002. Booklet $2.75. How to look for work in a traditional way: preparing a resume, writing letters of application, and job interviews.

Tips on Work-At-Home Schemes. Council of Better Business Bureaus, 1515 Wilson Blvd., Arlington, VA 22209; (703) 276-0100. Send $1 (with long SASE) for brochure that gives you the low-down about schemes taking advantage of folks answering classified ads or direct mail brochures. Gives advice on how to find out if such work-at-home offers are legitimate.

Working in Retirement. 50 Plus Guidebooks, 850 Third Av., New York, NY 10022; (212) 715-2787. Booklet, $3.50 (inc. postage and handling). Discusses ways of working, how and where to look for work, tax penalties of earning too much, and where to get training.

Park Service Offices

National Park Service Regional Offices

Contact these offices for information on specific volunteer programs.

North Atlantic—15 State St., Boston, MA 02109 (Connecticut, Maine, Massachusetts, New Hampshire, New Jersey, New York, Rhode Island, and Vermont)

Mid-Atlantic—143 S. Third St., Philadelphia, PA 19106 (Pennsylvania, Maryland, West Virginia, Delaware, and Virginia, excluding parks assigned to National Capital Region)

National Capital—1100 Ohio Dr. SW, Washington, DC 20242 (Metropolitan area of Washington, DC, with some areas in Maryland, Virginia, and West Virginia)

Southeast—75 Spring St. SW, Atlanta, GA 30303 (Alabama, Florida, Georgia, Kentucky, Mississippi, North Carolina, South Carolina, Tennessee, Puerto Rico, and the Virgin Islands)

Rocky Mountain—655 Parfet St., Box 25287, Denver, CO 80225; (303) 234-3095

Utah—P.O. Box 11505, Salt Lake City, UT 84111; (801) 524-5311

Southwest—Old Santa Fe Trail, Box 728, Santa Fe, NM 87501; (505) 988-6340

West—450 Golden Gate Av., San Francisco, CA 94012; (415) 556-4122

Oregon—P.O. Box 2965, 729 NE Oregon St., Portland, OR; (503) 234-3361, Ext 4024

Pacific Northwest—Pike Bldg., 1424 Fourth Av., Seattle, WA 98101; (206) 442-5542

State Parks Offices

Contact these offices for information on specific volunteer programs.

Alaska Division of Parks—323 E. Fourth Av., Anchorage, AK 99501; (907) 274-4676

Arizona Park Board—1688 W. Adams, Phoenix, AZ 85007; (602) 271-4174

California Dept of Parks & Rec.—P.O. Box 2390, Sacramento, CA 95811; (916) 445-6477

Idaho Dept. of Parks—Capitol Building, Boise, ID 83720; (208) 384-2154

Nevada State Parks System—210 S. Fall St. #221, Carson City, NV 89701; (702) 885-4370

Oregon State Parks—300 State Highway Bldg., Salem, OR 97301

Utah Division of Parks & Rec.—1596 W. North Temple, Salt Lake City, UT 84116; (801) 328-6011

Index

About the Author

John Howells is the author of seven books on retirement strategies and locations in the United States and abroad. His writing on this subject has been praised by reviewers in many of the country's leading newspapers and magazines. He and his wife, Sherry, travel back and forth across the United States by automobile, motorhome and airplane to conduct their research. They talk with innumerable retirees and visit senior citizens' centers, chambers of commerce, newspaper offices—anywhere they can get current information on retirement lifestyles.

John is increasingly in demand as the author of magazine articles and as a speaker in symposia on the subject of affordable retirement. He continues to defer his own retirement and is currently developing a series of regional retirement guides, starting with one on the Southwest due in the spring of 1996.

To order direct, send check or money order to:
Gateway Books, 2023 Clemens Road, Oakland CA 94602

Adventures Abroad $12.95.................................. $_____

Choose Costa Rica $13.95.................................... _____

Choose Mexico $11.95... _____

Choose Spain $11.95... _____

Get Up & Go $10.95.. _____

Retirement on a Shoestring $8.95........................ _____

RV Travel in Mexico $9.95.................................... _____

Where to Retire $14.95....... **NEW EDITION**..............._____

Postage & Handling
First book.............................$1.90   _____
Each additional book..........1.00   _____
California residents add 8% sales tax   _____

Total $ _____

( ) I enclose my check or money order
( ) Please charge my credit card

Visa   Master Card   American Express

#_____Exp. Date _____

Name on Card _____

Telephone (   )_____
Please ship to:

Name_____

Address_____

City/State/Zip_____

Our books are shipped bookrate. Please allow 2 - 3 weeks for delivery. If you are not satisfied, the price of the book(s) will be refunded in full. (U. S. funds for all orders, please.)